# Existential Group Counselling and Psychotherapy

I0025361

*Existential Group Counselling and Psychotherapy* provides a theoretical and practical foundation for practice, including a solid grounding in the 'why' and 'how' of therapeutic groupwork from an existential perspective.

The first part of the book, 'Modern western origins', offers a review of modern western sources: a survey of early developments, what formats have endured, and to what extent these antecedents have informed, but are distinct from, current paradigms. The second part, 'Being and doing', provides a description of the existential phenomenological paradigm for group therapeutic groupwork, reviewing possible therapeutic effects, as well as risks and disappointments that may affect both members, and facilitators. Part three, 'Doing and being', covers practice, procedure, and possible problems.

Written in a practical, accessible style, and incorporating clinical vignettes and anecdotal material, the book will be relevant for counsellors and psychotherapists in training and practice, as well as for special interest organisations that sponsor groups.

**Karen Weixel-Dixon** is a psychotherapist, supervisor, and accredited mediator in private practice, and a visiting lecturer at Regent's University London. Her paradigm is existential phenomenological, and she is particularly interested in how people experience, and engage with, time.

# Existential Group Counselling and Psychotherapy

Authored by Karen Weixel-Dixon

Routledge
Taylor & Francis Group

LONDON AND NEW YORK

First published 2020
by Routledge
2 Park Square, Milton Park, Abingdon, Oxon OX14 4RN

and by Routledge
52 Vanderbilt Avenue, New York, NY 10017

Routledge is an imprint of the Taylor & Francis Group, an informa business

British Library Cataloguing-in-Publication Data
A catalogue record for this book is available from the British Library

Library of Congress Cataloging-in-Publication Data
A catalog record for this book has been requested

ISBN: 978-0-367-02556-4 (hbk)
ISBN: 978-0-367-02988-3 (pbk)
ISBN: 978-0-429-02011-7 (ebk)

Typeset in Times New Roman
by Apex CoVantage, LLC

To my wonderful husband Neil, whose support never fails.

# Contents

# Introduction

This book seeks to provide a foundation in the principles that underpin existential group counselling and psychotherapy.

Many of the tenets reviewed here will be supported by anecdotal accounts that serve to illuminate the points made: these scenarios should be taken not as factual reports but rather as representations of common occurrences.

The distinction between counselling and psychotherapy is, for this practitioner, indiscernible; however, many in the field describe the former project as one likely to be goal focused and time-limited, while the latter is more likely to address long-term difficulties and 'deep-rooted' issues. All of these elements will be considered and discussed in a manner that will, hopefully, be useful for both perspectives.

Additionally, there is a rationale for time-limited work in Part III that is grounded in existential principles, and can be pertinent for any model of the helping professions.

The first part of the book, 'Modern western origins', is a brief review of modern western sources: a survey of early developments, what formats have endured, and to what extent these antecedents have informed, but are distinct from, current paradigms.

Part II, 'Being and doing', provides a description of the existential phenomenological paradigm for group therapeutic groupwork. The distinguishing characteristics of this model are elucidated and the possible implications for the process introduced. The emphasis here is on how to understand inter-subjective processes, how the world-views of members are structured and inter-related, and how the contributions of phenomenology and its associated methodology inform the project of therapy.

Once this perspective is described, the suitability of this model for groupwork is clarified.

Additionally, this section reviews possible therapeutic effects, as well as risks and disappointments that may affect both members and facilitators.

Finally, this discussion concludes with a description of the responsibilities of the facilitator, the members, and the group.

Part III, titled 'Doing and Being', covers practice, procedure, and possible problems.

The 'Doing' of existential therapy is grounded in the 'Being' of those involved: there is discussion here about the nature of 'dialogue', rather than technique, and a number of communication options reflect this premise. These possibilities reflect the 'art' of listening, exploring, and responding, a cycle of clarification and understanding that can continue indefinitely.

This section also offers some perspectives on difficult or challenging behaviours, a model for working with dreams, some points for the culmination of the group, and some considerations for an ethical framework.

This text is not meant to be a 'how to' manual: the proposals here are meant to deepen understanding of the *possibilities* inherent in the practice of existential group psychotherapy. Each practitioner will bring their own understandings to bear on the work; this is as it should be, as this endeavour is more art than science and is, therefore, a creative and sometimes chaotic endeavour.

As Yalom asserts,

> The vast bulk of therapy cannot be systematically described.
>
> (Yalom, 1995, p. 325)

This text will be most readily relevant to those groups formed to explore, negotiate, and implement change; most of the theoretical proposals considered here would be applicable to in-patient situations as well as out-patient. However, even when therapeutic results are not a specific aim, many of the perspectives presented are certainly pertinent to family, social, professional, and cultural groupings. Hopefully, these principles can provide some understanding of what issues and themes are in effect.

There will be a summary and conclusion to the proposals and discussions presented in each part of the text.

## Reference

Yalom, I.D. *The Theory and Practice of Group Psychotherapy*, 1995, Basic Books, New York.

# Part I

# Modern western origins

# Chapter 1

# Historical overview

We humans seem to prefer clear dichotomies to ambiguous positions: black and white, right and wrong, true and false, winning and losing, and, perhaps the most significant divide for a conscious being, life and death.

Dichotomies seem to present us with clear pictures, leaving little room for debate or uncertainty: they make our choices 'easier'. This proposal will be the subject of a later discussion about the human predicament and how we engage with the condition of uncertainty.

The historical development of group models, indeed of psychotherapy as a whole, reflects at least three classical dichotomies: nurture/nature, inside/outside, and individual/group.

Some basic considerations reflected in these questions might be inferred. Are we (each) a product of innate nature, that is, inherent personal characteristics, or of the external forces of nurture, as in the social and familial impositions to which we are subjected? Is there a 'self', an entity 'inside', completely separate, though related to the 'outside', which is everything and everyone else? And which configuration is primary, the individual or the 'group' (family, society, etc.)?

It is likely that proponents of both the humanistic and the psychodynamic schools of thought would recognise proposals such as 'the true self lies within', or 'be your own person', or 'authenticity requires one to be true to themselves'; these perspectives give priority to the individual 'inside'. A corollary of this view is that one's authenticity can be compromised by conceding to public dictates or the expectations of others.

Similarly, the psychodynamic paradigms are generally inclined to address that which is 'inside': the unconscious is a repository of truth as well as fiction, although it is also proposed that neither of these perspectives is readily accessible to the being to which they belong.

Additionally, the nature/nurture polarity is generally applied in support of the orthodoxy that 'nature' reflects what is 'natural', or 'real', and is therefore (more) genuine than 'nurture', which is represented in culture-bound values and therefore subjective and possibly ambiguous.

It has been suggested that the positions described here are not exclusively 'either/or'; there can be a 'dialectic between the seeming polarities, as Dalal suggests:

> Thus the Freudian schema is . . . a complicated dialectic between the inside and the outside.
>
> (Dalal, 1998, p. 18)

It should be noted, however, that rather than dispute that divide, this is a comment on the connection between the subdivisions.

Certainly, all three dualities noted here seem to imply that the individual, related to but separate from the outer world, is more fundamental than the group.

One's perspective on these issues will, to a large extent, be reflected in the paradigm of choice for group counselling and psychotherapy. Most models favour the view that the group is a collection of individuals; the existential phenomenological paradigm challenges the very notion of 'individual', as we shall see.

These themes will be further elucidated in the following chapters on the early pioneers of groupwork and the development of their approaches: Chapter 2, Kurt Lewin; Chapter 3, Wilfred Bion; Chapter 4, S.H. Foulkes; Chapter 5, Carl Rogers; and Chapter 6, Irvin D. Yalom.

The second section will also review a small part of the numerous historical precedents that gave rise to the appreciation of group psychotherapy and counselling as practices that are equally effective as that of individual therapy. The reigning view prior to the more modern developments was that group therapy was a concession to limited resources, like time, money, and trained personnel, and could not provide the therapeutic effects expected with traditional models.

The work of five seminal theorists and practitioners will be reviewed in brief, and the move from institutionalised, organisational, and learning focused groupwork to psychotherapeutic frameworks will be traced through their efforts and contributions.

These are not the only contributors, but rather are those that, in my estimation, demonstrate how the humanistic approach was appreciated by analytical theorists, and how it gradually informed and shaped groupwork prior to it being appreciated as a paradigm in its own right.

The review of principles that were tried, discarded, retained, and revised is also interesting in terms of current thought and practice.

## Reference

Dalal, F. *Taking the Group Seriously*, 1998, Jessica Kingsley Publishers, London.

# Chapter 2

# Kurt Lewin (1890–1947)

Kurt Lewin was born in Prussia, one of four siblings in a Jewish family. His university studies were diverse: medicine, philosophy, psychology. He didn't complete his PhD at the University of Berlin until after his service in WWI.

Lewin immigrated to the United States in 1933, where he worked at Cornell University and for the Child Welfare Research Station at the University of Iowa. It was under the auspices of this latter organisation that he constructed an experiment in association with R. Lippitt and R.K. White that demonstrated the effects upon children, in the age range of 10 and 11 years, of 'democratic' and 'authoritarian' group leadership styles.

Lewin offers this description of the autocratic leadership style:

> the autocratic atmosphere gives a much greater and aggressive dominance of the leader, and a narrowing down of the free movement of the members.
>
> (Lewin, 1948, p. 77)

The leader in this role would decide, for example, who could work with whom; he would set specific goals and specify exactly how these were to be accomplished. He would critically evaluate the results without stating the reason or evidence of the qualification.

The democratic leader would allow the group to determine policy and procedure. Members were free to work with whomever they chose. The leader would be more of a participant in the group processes, without taking over the actual work; he offered praise with justification.

The results of this project were significant on many levels.

In terms of how the children related to each other: in the autocratic group, children were more hostile, aggressive, divisive, and competitive. In the democratic group, children were more deferential to each other, more cooperative, and more creative, and their language reflected more 'we' statements as opposed to the 'I'-focused statements noted in the other group.

In terms of how the children related to the leaders in each group: in the autocratic group, the children's approach to the leader was submissive and more frequently initiated by the children compared to the democratic group, and they were less likely to offer alternatives means of implementing plans to those specified by the leader.

In the democratic group, the children demonstrated a more independent relationship and sought input from the leader less frequently; they were more likely to bond among themselves rather than seek attention from the leader.

It was clear the leadership style affected the relationships among the children as much as their relationship to the leader.

There was a further observation with reference to the notion of power within the two groups: as the children in the autocratic group had no possibility of acquiring any status or power in their group, they resorted to scapegoating a member. Lewin comments:

> In other words, every child became a potential enemy of every other one . . . through combining in an attack against one individual the members who otherwise could not gain higher status were able to do so by violent suppression of one of their fellows.
>
> (ibid., p. 80)

In the authoritarian group, the children experienced a limited amount of personal power and sought to impose their will on each other.

In the democratic group, it appeared that the power was shared, but not necessarily equally or consistently.

In an effort to address objections that these results were merely a matter of individual propensities, one child from each group was transferred to the other; it was but a short while before the children's behaviour changed in accordance with the group to which they were relocated.

This experiment prompted consideration about leadership styles and their effects, an important factor with respect to any facilitated group endeavour.

In reviewing the findings of this experiment, Lewin states:

> The group to which a child belongs is the ground on which he stands . . . the group the person is a part of, and the culture in which he lives, determine to a very high degree his behaviour and character.
>
> (ibid., p. 82)

This proposal, extended to adults as well, underpins the subsequent work and findings pursued and offered by Lewin and his associates' some of these became premises for a more inter-personal exercise, which in turn paved the way for the basis of psychotherapeutic approach.

The results of the experiment in Iowa, along with subsequent findings, clarified one of the most well known of Lewin's proposals, that of the 'field theory', which Cohn describes:

> Lewin's 'field theory' proposes that each individual exists in a psychological field of forces that determines his or her behaviour . . . the emphasis here is on

the total situation, on interaction rather than the co-existence of self-sufficient entities.

(Cohn, 1997, p. 48)

Lewin assents:

all actions are based on the ground the person happens to stand upon. . . . The firmness of his actions and the clearness of his decisions depend largely upon the stability of this 'ground'.

(Lewin, 1948, p. 145)

As noted earlier, the ground to which Lewin refers is the group, or groups, that a person claims affiliation with, or 'belongs' to. The 'figure' is the individual, who stands as both a part-of and apart-from the background; and although an inherent aspect of the whole, the background is often subjugated.

It must be noted, in the quote cited, that Lewin assigns a primary position to the group: the essential condition is described as a 'with-world' in existential literature.

This concept also resonates with the 'matrix' as described by Foulkes, which will be discussed further, and with many of the existential notions of inter-relational and inter-subjective conditions that are outlined in later chapters of this text: Chapter 12, Relatedness; Chapter 21, The contributions of existential phenomenology; and Chapter 24, Relational issues.

Lewin went on to develop a model of learning and development known as the 'T Group', or training group.

Organised in 1946, this first project was intended to provide training to leaders in a government office. The small groups were primarily discussion groups in the first instance. The exchanges between all participants were monitored and annotated by the group leaders and observers and were discussed subsequent to each session.

When those involved as group members learned of these reviews, they requested the opportunity to attend; it was, by all accounts, a dramatic event (Yalom, 1995).

The occasion to hear one's behaviour scrutinised, reported, and considered with respect to the effects was a novel experience. Eventually, the participants of the groups were encouraged to give their responses to the observations and comments offered by the facilitators as well as to those offered by their peers during the session; thus was introduced the exchange now known as 'feedback'.

The information as to how each of them was being experienced by the others, as well as the analysis of their exchanges reported by the observers, and the dynamic of in situ feedback provided a new understanding for the participants as to their manner of relating and communicating.

Yalom comments:

The staff immediately recognised that they had . . . discovered a powerful technique of human relations: *experiential learning*. Group members learn most effectively by studying the very interactional network in which they are enmeshed.

(Yalom, 1995, p. 487)

Lewin was known for keeping meticulous records of his research, which was useful for tracing the development of his methods and their effects.

There were numerous experiments that supported, and extended, the early findings of that innovative project. The purpose of the T-group became less an educational enterprise and more an inter-relational and psychotherapeutic exercise.

Another of Lewin's key theoretical proposals that found its way into modern psychotherapeutic models is that of 'interdependence of fate'. This premise also provides an interesting definition of a 'group':

> It is not similarity or dissimilarity of individuals that constitutes a group, but rather the interdependence of fate . . . a person who has learned to see how much his own fate depends on the fate of his entire group will be ready and even eager to take over a fair share of responsibility for its welfare.
>
> (British Library, 2018)

It might be understood from this statement that by definition a 'group' shares an assignment, a 'task' of some sort, or even multiple tasks; furthermore, what is notable about the proposal is the necessity of cooperation from others in realising these goals.

However, Lewin pointed out that there is always a tension between the aims of the group and those of the individual. In his seminal text, *Resolving Social Conflicts* (1948), Lewin is clear that groups (family, social, therapeutic) function *best* when there are elements of tension and conflict. One might infer that this certainly made a case for the promotion of diversity.

The influence of the Gestalt school of psychology is also represented in Lewin's application of figure/ground formation.

He comments:

> Every action one performs has some specific 'background', and is *determined* by that background. . . . Experiments have shown how important the background is for any perception. . . . They have also proved that the background itself is not often perceived, but only the 'figure' or 'event'.
>
> (ibid., p. 145, italics mine)

Again, what is particularly striking about the latter assertion is the significance of the background, which is the group; as in the symbol Taijitu, commonly referred to as the Yin and Yang, there is an 'embeddedness' that defies separate identification of the parts.

This, as we shall see, is a view echoed in the existential phenomenological literature, particularly with respect to the inter-relatedness of self and other, as well as the issue of responsibility that extends indefinitely.

To conclude this brief review of Lewin's contributions to the field of psycho-therapeutic thinking, we will consider one of the premises most readily associated with Lewin, which extends the description and function of a group as indicated earlier:

> It is today widely recognised that a group is more than, or, more exactly, different from, the sum of its members. . . . A group can be characterised as a 'dynamical whole'; this means that a change in the state of any subpart changes the state of any other subpart.
>
> (Lewin, 1948, p. 84)

This postulate is one that was first promoted by Gestalt psychologists, with whom Lewin studied at the Berlin Psychological Institute, notably Wolfgang Kohler and Max Wertheimer (Cohn, 1997).

This view suggests that the whole, the group, is something other than a collection of individuals; it would therefore be less effective to 'apply' techniques that promote an analysis of the individual as an entity unto itself, or to employ strategies unrelated to the relational processes of the group.

By virtue of the principles outlined here, it would seem that Lewin embraces the notion of the integration of outside/inside, as well as that of individual and group: consequently, with reference to the nature/nurture dichotomy, the 'nurture' aspect of existence is favoured as the dominant source, and force, for behaviour.

Lewin's work influenced theories in organisational dynamics and supported novel perspectives in sociological and psychological theses. His research provided a grounded opposition to the applied psychoanalytical model that embraced notions of the primacy of the individual and the attending notions that held sway in the early development of psychotherapeutic groupwork.

His views informed and supported what was at that time a nascent existential phenomenological perspective on the therapeutic project and the appreciation of the inter-subjective condition of human existence.

## References

British Library. Kurt Lewin, 2018, available at www.bl.uk/people/kurt-lewin, accessed 22 July 2018.

Cohn, H.W. *Existential Thought and Therapeutic Practice*, 1997, Sage Publications, London.

Lewin, K., *Resolving Social Conflicts*, 1948 (ed. G. Lewin), Harper and Brothers Publishers, New York.

Yalom, I. *The Theory and Practice of Group Psychotherapy*, 1995, Basic Books, New York.

# Chapter 3

# Wilfred Bion (1897–1979)

Bion was born in India but educated in Great Britain, where he studied medicine at University College, London. He subsequently trained for seven years in psychoanalysis at the Tavistock Clinic in London and was in analysis with Melanie Klein. During the Second World War, Bion worked with traumatised soldiers in military hospitals, including the Northfield Military Hospital in Birmingham, in the company of S.H. Foulkes and Patrick de Maré.

Bion is known for having developed a paradigm for group therapy known as the 'Tavistock method'. Although this method, as it was widely practised in the 1970s and 1980s, has fallen from favour, Bion's work is significant for its style of leadership, which might be described as aloof and impersonal, and for the notion of a 'group mind' or 'group culture'. Both elements lent themselves readily to the application of psychodynamic theory and procedure in a group setting, especially as they related to the key principle of transference.

Bion's opening chapter to his text *Experiences in Groups and Other Papers* (1961) is titled: 'Intra-group tensions in therapy: their study as the task of the group' (Bion, 1961, p. 11).

When the group operated within this task, their communications had a 'present' focus; the communications were less ambiguous and clearly addressed current obstacles to the stated aim.

The group was considered to be working effectively when this task was being pursued, but there an impediment to this aim was frequently displayed that took the form of one of three basic assumptions (or emotional states) on the part of the group: the basic assumption of dependence; the basic assumption of pairing, and the basic assumption of fight/flight (Bion, 1961).

The first of these three was characterised by the group's hope and expectation that the leader would take care of their individual needs for safety and emotional sustenance. The second is characterised by the notion that a sub-group, a pair of any gender, will produce a new leader that will satisfy their expectations. The third is characterised by a fear of something threatening that must be dealt with by the strategy of fight, or flight, and this choice is one to be made by an all-knowing leader.

It is clear that all three conditions are directly related to the group leader; as such, they are ripe for classic transference interpretations.

In individual psychoanalysis, interpretation is a technique employed in the analysis of transference from the patient to the analyst:

> Transference . . . refers to the client's unconscious shifting to the therapist . . . of feelings, attitudes, and fantasies (both positive and negative) that stem from reactions to significant persons from the client's past . . . usually childhood ones.
>
> (Corey, 2004, p. 144)

It is proposed that an effective interpretation (of transference, dreams, and resistances) will produce a novel understanding, for the patient, of the patient's predicament and behaviour.

Freud writes:

> We overcome the transference by pointing to the patient that his feelings . . . do not apply to the person of the doctor, but that they are repeating something that happened to him earlier. In this way we oblige him to transform his repetition into a memory.
>
> (Freud, 1991, p. 496)

If this is accomplished, it is supposed that the patient will be able, in the context of analysis, to work through the conflicts and disappointments experienced in early relationships and achieve a more satisfactory resolution: they will no longer be hampered by illusions.

But who or what is being analysed in a group situation? In Bion's model, it is the group as a whole:

> I have suggested that it helped to elucidate the tensions of the group to suppose the existence of a group mentality. This term I use to describe what I believe to be the unanimous expression of the will of the group, an expression of will to which individuals contribute anonymously.
>
> (Bion, 1992, p. 59)

The function of interpretation is to clarify the distortions imposed by the patient (i.e., the group) onto the therapist, particularly with reference to the three basic assumptions as shown. To the extent that the group is satisfied with this explanation, it is hoped it will transition into a working group again . . . and this cycle of therapeutic work, and interference, may continue indefinitely.

It should be noted also that transference is the mechanism by which an individual 'projects' onto another person the assumptions that they hold 'inside' their psyche: the inside informs the behaviour on the 'outside'.

Thus, the group would be addressed as a single entity; no questions from individual members would be recognised. Communication between members was not recognised or worked with. The therapist would clarify the theme, present it in the form of interpretation, and demonstrate how each member participates in its construction.

The concept of transference required a particular kind, or lack, of engagement on the part of the analyst:

> The less the therapist's real self appears, the more readily does the patient transfer onto him feelings that belong elsewhere.
>
> (Yalom, 1980, p. 412)

This maxim may go some way in explaining Bion's impassive demeanour, as he adhered to the policies of psychodynamic practice.

This notion of the group as singular entity supports another of Bion's fundamental tenets:

> there is no way in which the individual can, in a group, 'do nothing' – not even by doing nothing. So we have come round once more, though from a different angle, to our suspicion that all members of a group are responsible for the behaviour of the group.
>
> (ibid., p. 118)

This idea has a definite resonance with issues of responsibility as proposed in existential literature, to be reviewed subsequently. In Bion's work, it indicates that each individual inevitably brings some kind of expectation or attitude to the group context that informs the 'group mentality'. This is considered to be one of his most significant insights and resonates with humanistic models in their appreciation of the inter-personal dynamics of groupwork, and of life.

Bion's work warrants some credit for its descriptions of groups that seemingly sabotage their own purpose: individuals seek a leader that will assuage their anxieties, keep them safe, alleviate the burden of responsibility, and help to mitigate the negative consequences of change. Although these strategies were couched in psychodynamic terms in his written works, they are probably readily observable to group facilitators or leaders in any collective gathering: teams, societies, communes, or university training programs.

It is also noteworthy that Bion described 'frustration' as the most common emotional experience in groupwork; the patient always finds it difficult to balance the intentions of the working group with his own needs and wants. There is always a tension. This insight is frequently observable in the behaviour and narrative of group members and within any kind of organised congregation.

Studies in social sciences and organisational psychology also owe a debt to his view that we are, inevitably, always a part of a group:

> No individual, however isolated in time and space, should be regarded as outside a group or lacking in active manifestations of group psychology.
>
> (Bion, 1992, p. 169)

But for Bion, as well as for those who adhered to Freud's theories, the individual was the primary entity:

> A psychological group is a collection of individuals who have introduced the same person into their superego . . . and have identified themselves with one another in their ego.
>
> (Freud, 1933, p. 67)

Additionally, the basic assumption group, of all types formerly described, is regarded as

> a timeless, instinctive, and emotional state.
>
> (Bion, 1992, p. 168)

This is in keeping with the proposals of Melanie Klein (1882–1960), with whom Bion was in analysis for some years while at the Tavistock, and whose theories about infant development focused on primitive drives and instinctive impulses.

This latter proposal also indicates the nature and effect of interpretation in Bion's model: to make conscious the unconscious psychotic and primitive phantasies, thereby freeing the client to embrace a more 'realistic' understanding of their current situation, and to become aware of how adhering to such projections protects them from conscious awareness and, ultimately, estranges them from personal responsibility for their life.

This, too, locates Bion on the 'nature' side of the 'nature/nurture' divide, as well as favouring the 'inside' of the inside/outside dichotomy.

The model employed by Bion is no longer popular, but his writings, quirky, personal, and sometimes enigmatic, bestowed a number of insights that are certainly still relevant. Examples of these include: there is inevitably a conflict between an individual's needs and desires with those of the group, and each member must relegate some aspirations in order to enjoy the benefits of the group projects; the group can satisfy certain values, such as belonging to something greater than oneself, in a way that solitary existence cannot (if such a thing were possible); and the fundamental task of the group is to explore intra-group tensions.

Although these tenets are sourced in the analytical model espoused by Bion, they accord with humanistic and existential thought, as we shall see.

## References

Bion, W.R. *Experiences in Groups*, (1961) 1992, Routledge, London and New York.
Corey, G. *Theory and Practice of Group Counselling*, 2004, Brooks/Cole, Belmont, CA.
Freud, S. *New Introductory Lectures on Psychoanalysis*, 1933, Hogarth Press, London.
Freud, S. *Introductory Lectures on Psychoanalysis*, 1991 (trans. James Strachey), Penguin, London.
Yalom, I. *Existential Psychotherapy*, 1980, Basic Books, New York.

# Chapter 4

# S.H. Foulkes (1898–1976)

Foulkes was a German-British psychoanalyst and psychiatrist. He studied at the Frankfurt Neurological Institute; while there, he came under the influence of Kurt Goldstein, whose ideas were rooted in Gestalt psychology and phenomenology (Cohn, 1997).

Foulkes immigrated to London in 1933, where he founded the Group Analytic Society and was instrumental in establishing the Institute of Group Analysis. He was subsequently drafted into the British Army and posted in 1944 to Northfield Military Hospital in Birmingham, England, which specialised in trauma and neurosis. Here he worked alongside Wilfred Bion and Patrick de Maré in the establishment of the first therapeutic community.

Foulkes had studied the works of Freud, but he made a radical departure from many of those theories at an early stage in his practice. He distanced himself from basic psychoanalytical tenets:

> the bottom line in Freud is that he gives ontological priority to the internal over the external, to the biological over the social, and to the individual over the group.
>
> (Dalal, 1998, p. 32)

In contrast to this, Foulkes stated categorically:

> Each individual – itself an artificial, though plausible, abstraction – is basically and centrally determined, inevitably, by the world in which he lives, by the community, the group, of which he forms a part.
>
> (Foulkes, 1983, p. 10)

This assertion is aligned with a recognised phenomenological view that informed Foulkes' model for groupwork: that human existence is fundamentally relational.

At Northfield, the entire hospital – staff, doctors, patients, service providers – became a 'coherent, but not an "organised body"' (Foulkes, 1975, p. 9), where free communication was favoured among all parties. Even those patients in the reception area were requested to 'free associate' among themselves, to share, in that brief interval, their thoughts, hopes, and anxieties.

This setting was a paradigm of what Foulkes viewed as the 'matrix', reminiscent of Lewin's 'field theory' and also akin to the Gestalt notion of figure/ground configurations (we must recall his association with Goldstein in Frankfurt). The entire hospital, in this instance, was the 'ground', and the individuals were the 'figures' in the network.

'Network' was also a term employed by Foulkes:

> The term *network* was used to express the fact that our individual patient is, in essence, merely a symptom of a disturbance of equilibrium in the intimate network of which he is a part.
>
> (ibid., p. 12)

This principle suggests that problems are shared by the network; the source of the disturbance is within the group. Again, this displayed favour for the outside of the inside/outside dichotomy.

In Foulkes' better-known works, the concept of the inherent relationship of individual and group is most often referred to as a 'matrix':

> The network of all individual mental processes, the psychological medium in which they meet, communicate, and interact, can be called the matrix.
>
> (Foulkes and Anthony, 1965, p. 26)

These phenomenological ideas will be discussed in depth later in this text, but it is important to note that Kurt Goldstein, whose lectures Foulkes attended, was an acknowledged source of influence on Foulkes' theoretical tenets (Cohn, 1997).

In brief, the results of the Northfield project were dramatic. Foulkes and the team were able to observe and interact with more soldiers more frequently; the soldiers fared better with this model than those receiving more traditional psychotherapeutic treatment. Perhaps most significantly, 'it became apparent that the subtle but vital phenomenon of morale, involving the whole ward, was promoted. . . . It had a totalising, as distinct from fragmenting and isolating, effect' (De Maré, 2012, p. 24).

This was an early experiment in group analytic psychotherapy, a practice in which Foulkes had been engaged since 1940. He did issue a caveat, however, with respect to groups organised within institutions, i.e., large groups, that these networks should be encouraged to maintain a focus on the problems shared within the specified context, thus creating a 'therapeutic community'. This would differ from groups of unconnected individuals who convene for specific tasks: the latter category could sit on 'a continuum from therapeutic to learning processes' (Foulkes, 1975, p. 6).

He did offer in another passage a seemingly more inclusive view with reference to the general principles applicable to groupwork:

> the principles developed and maintained . . . in the therapeutic group-analytic group can be applied to all forms of human groups even if they are not primarily therapeutic.
>
> (ibid., p. 4)

This is recognised as a contribution from Foulkes that influenced the fields of social psychology, organisational psychology, and social anthropology.

The phenomenological and existential themes found in Foulkes' theories were expanded upon in subsequent written works, although it has been suggested that he demonstrated some ambivalence towards the psychoanalytic approach throughout his career (Cohn, 1997; Dalal, 1998).

However, he is remembered for his insistence on the group as the primary unit and on the inter-relational condition of human existence. These concepts place him firmly in the camp that eschews the inside/outside, nature/nurture, and individual/group divides as specious.

The phenomenological precepts espoused in Foulkes' work could be summarised:

> The group is the ontological unit: individual and group are semantic conveniences; the whole is other than the sum of its parts; the individual (in essence) cannot be extracted from a/the context, and the context is qualitatively something other than the compilation of individuals.

The part is always in relation to a whole, and the whole is related to other wholes, and this connection proceeds indefinitely: this represents the interconnectedness of all human existence, past, present, and future.

In refutation of the Cartesian duality generally assumed by other models of psychology, he states:

> The 'mind' is not represented by what's inside a person: 'The mind that is usually called intrapsychic is a property of the group, *and the processes that take place are due to the dynamic interactions in this communicational matrix*'.
>
> (Foulkes, 1990, p. 278, italics mine)

This further suggests that 'Foulkes saw psychological disturbance as a disturbance of communication, a kind of extreme individualism that rejects contact with others' (Cohn, 1997, p. 51).

It follows, then, that working towards an ever more articulate form of communication is identical to the therapeutic process itself (Foulkes, 1983, p. 168).

Communication unfettered by social constraints, and free of manipulative intent, is meant to be the aspiration of group members; in this manner, the members come to know themselves better, as their appreciation and understanding of others changes and deepens.

Finally, Foulkes comments:

> Group-analytic psychotherapy . . . is a form of psychotherapy *by* the group, *of* the group, including its conductor.
>
> (Foulkes, 1975, p. 3)

More will be said of this when the functions of the facilitator and the group members are discussed, but it is important to note here that the therapist/facilitator makes it clear that he is an interactive member of the network, and that the 'work' of the group is the responsibility of that matrix.

The work by the group can include any kind of observations, interpretations, questions, explorations, or selection of topics, or silence. These are possibilities open to all members and should only be offered by the 'conductor' (Foulkes' word for facilitator) when he believes there is a blockage in communication; that is, when the group seems to be impeded in its efforts to effectively communicate.

In keeping with the notion of a group matrix, comments may be directed to individuals or to the group as a whole. In either case, the expressions will have an effect on and for the whole group.

Foulkes' commitment to group analysis as the most effective mode of psychological work is summarised in his assertion:

> it would be true to say that group psychotherapy is indicated whenever psychotherapy is indicated.
>
> (Foulkes, 1986, p. 65)

## References

Cohn, H.W. *Existential Thought and Therapeutic Practice*, 1997, Sage Publications, London.

Dalal, F. *Taking the Group Seriously*, 1998, Jessica Kingsley Publishers Ltd., London.

De Maré, P. 'Michael Foulkes and the Northfield Experiment', in *Small, Large, and Median Groups*, 2012 (eds. R. Lenn and K. Stefano), p. 24, Karnac, London.

Foulkes, S.H. *Group Analytic Psychotherapy*, 1986, Karnac, London.

———. *Introduction to Group Analytic Psychotherapy: Studies in the Social Integration of Individuals and Groups*, 1983, Karnac, London.

———. *Selected Papers*, 1990 (ed. E. Foulkes), Karnac, London.

Foulkes, S.H., and Anthony, E.J. *Group Psychotherapy, the Psychoanalytic Approach*, 1965, Karnac, London.

# Chapter 5

# Carl Rogers (1902–1987)

Rogers was born in Chicago to a religious fundamentalist family; he later abandoned his beliefs and became an atheist. He studied at Columbia University, where he completed his M.A. and doctorate.

Rogers was a prolific writer and published joint works and developed programs with Eugene T. Gendlin ('focusing' paradigm) and Abraham Maslow, among others. He was considered the leading theorist and practitioner of what became the 'person-centered' model of therapy and counselling.

In accordance with his proposal that the human being is a self-actualising organism, the responsibility of the therapist in group settings was to provide an atmosphere that would best facilitate this natural tendency; the 'being' qualities of the therapist were emphasised over the 'doing' practicalities of the role (we will see that this view is shared by the existential phenomenological model that will be outlined subsequently).

Considering the manner of participation with reference to the therapist, Rogers notes:

> My hope is gradually to become as much a participant in the group as a facilitator.
>
> (Rogers, 1970, p. 51)

Extending this notion of egalitarian relationship, the first of the 'necessary and sufficient' conditions a therapist offers as a way of being in both group and individual contexts is 'congruence', or genuine presence; the second condition is empathy, which is a communicated desire and attempt to understand the client's perspective; and the final recommendation is unconditional positive regard, which is an appreciation and respect for the client's way of being.

The qualities referenced are readily understood, but empathy is an attitude that can be particularly difficult to explain, so we turn to Rogers for an apt review:

> Can I let myself enter fully into the world of his feelings and personal meanings and see these as he does? . . . I am often impressed with the fact that

even a minimal amount of empathic understanding – a bumbling and faulty attempt to catch the confused complexity of the client's meaning – is helpful.

(Rogers, 1961, p. 53)

Even a simply adequate understanding of another person's subjective experience and the communication of that understanding will, according to Rogers, promote in the client some self-acceptance, self-understanding, and a more appreciative (empathetic) attitude towards one-self as well as other people.

If these conditions are present, modelled by the therapist and, hopefully, provided to some degree by the group members, the obstacles to growth and self-actualisation will be mitigated.

This latter claim might serve as a summary of the aim of the work: it demonstrates a trust in the group process without a need for specific 'goals'. In fact, Rogers, to some large degree, eschews such intentions:

The group will *move* – of this I am confident – but it would be presumptuous to think that I can or should *direct* that movement.

(ibid., p. 50)

The 'T-Group', described earlier in this text, was originally employed primarily as an educational tool, with specific tasks; it was Rogers who took this idea further, with the emphasis on inter-personal learning, as well as a novel view on the kind of learning anticipated, that is, discovering, or uncovering, one's 'true self' and the development of one's inherent potential. Based on these principles, Rogers developed the format known as the 'encounter group'.

Yalom reminds us:

No historical account of the development and evolution of group therapy is complete without a description of the cross-fertilisation between the therapy and the encounter traditions.

(Yalom, 1995, p. 486)

Yalom professes an appreciation for the contributions of early encounter groups to the understanding and popularisation of inter-personal learning. He notes, however, a general distinction between the two practices: the therapy group is more often composed of people who are 'oriented towards survival rather than competence' (Yalom, 1995, p. 506).

Corey makes this observation about the overlap of the effects of the encounter group and the therapy group:

The basic encounter groups made it difficult to distinguish between 'therapy' and 'growth'.

(Corey, 2004, p. 271)

However, encounter groups, and intensive programs designed in the 1960s and 1970s for radical and quick routes to 'self-actualisation' or enhanced awareness (reflecting the 'excesses of pop culture'), began to lay claim to 'territory' that was previously the domain of psychotherapy and psychology. The reaction of the mental health profession was to pressure the government to pass legislation outlining the parameters of practice and the ethical and legal responsibilities for such projects, which were not professionally licensed and often were delivered by un-trained leaders.

The kind of 'growth' hoped for in the contemporary person-centred approach to group therapy might be summarised as an appreciation and realisation of one's own potential, which supports personal responsibility; congruence of self (the 'real' self) also contributes to self-direction, in that it implies the 'ownership' of one's feelings; and empathy produces an increased acceptance of one's own strengths and frailties as well as those of others and their situations, and a greater sense of openness and safety in relationships. These realisations result in behavioural adaptations that occur both within the group and in the members' wider inter-personal contacts.

However, the 'feel-good' factor of such aspirations is not sufficient in qualifying the group project as effective.

Rogers asserted:

> We do not believe that the group experience, no matter how uplifting, to be an end in itself, but find its significance primarily in the influence it has on later behaviour outside the group.
>
> (Rogers, 1970, p. 74)

Research at the time showed that these behaviours were almost inevitably re-enacted, adapted, and tested in the social, familial, and intimate associations, as well as in the organisational contexts of the group members (Rogers, 1970).

It may become apparent from the previous discussion regarding the aims and desired outcomes of person-centred theory that personal problems are seen as 'a fixity and remoteness of experience' (Rogers, 1961, p. 132). The client clings to historical behaviours and regimented ways of interpreting their experiences, refuses to allow genuine relating or communication, and often assigns responsibility for the quality of their experience to external sources. In this manner, the client impedes the natural growth processes and thereby avoids the anxiety that the prospect of change can provoke.

The core conditions outlined are referenced in some form in most humanistic paradigms (person-centred, Gestalt, existential), and the emphasis is on the positive impact of inter-personal relationships that operate with respect to these aspirations. These qualities are 'modelled' by the therapist and hopefully become appreciated and integrated into the attitudes and behaviour of the members once the therapeutic value has become apparent.

The person-centered approach is also based on a few key existential and phenomenological constructs: the subjective and conscious experience of the client is the principal arena for exploration, alongside those concerns common to all humans, such as freedom and responsibility, meaning, purpose, values, and authenticity. These are also prominent themes in existential thought and writings and will be extended and considered here in further detail in subsequent chapters: Chapter 14, Freedom and responsibility, and Chapter 16, Meaning, meaninglessness, nothingness.

However, the person-centered model is included in the category of 'humanistic' paradigms, which differs from existential phenomenological therapeutic models in a number of ways, including the distinction between inter-personal (the relations between distinct psyches) and inter-subjective (which indicates a fundamental relatedness), and in the notion of what is understood as the 'self'. In the person-centred approach, this latter concept is rooted in the designation of 'core self' and in the innate potentials for actualising this essence.

This commonly accepted view of the 'self' will be challenged in the following exposition on the existential phenomenological view of this concept.

Notably, with reference to the individual/group, inside/outside, nature/nurture dichotomies, it is apparent that the 'person-centred' paradigm favours those aspects that prioritise the individual over the group, the inherent possibilities 'inside' the person, as well as those inclinations designated as 'natural' in terms of 'becoming' a fulfilled human being. The impact of nature and nurture seem to be equitable: the 'natural' must be 'nurtured'.

Roger's contributions to the current models of group therapy are numerous. However, the view of the therapist as a participant/member who is a genuine and communicative part of the process and displays qualities of character, rather than expertise, is probably noted as one of the most valuable aspects of the paradigm.

Additionally, the paradigm's emphasis on 'being' qualities as opposed to 'doing' strategies is one shared by existential phenomenological practitioners, and will be reviewed at length in subsequent chapters: Chapter 21, The contributions of existential phenomenology and Chapter 22, The contributions of hermeneutics.

## References

Corey, G. *Theory and Practice of Group Counselling*, 2004, Thomson, Brooks/Cole, Belmont, CA, USA.

Rogers, C. *Encounter Groups*, 1970, Penguin, London, England.

———. *On Becoming a Person, a Therapist's View of Psychotherapy*, 1961, Constable, London.

Yalom, I. *The Theory and Practice of Group Psychotherapy*, 1995, Basic Books, New York.

# Chapter 6

# Irvin D. Yalom (1931–)

Yalom was born to Polish immigrant parents in Washington, D.C. He acquired a degree in medicine at Boston University; currently he is Professor Emeritus of Psychiatry at Stanford University School of Medicine.

Yalom's inimitable tome, *The Theory and Practice of Group Psychotherapy* (1995), is a scholarly work supported by extensive research findings and clinical material and is probably the most commonly referenced text on the subject. He has additionally published a number of books on the topics of therapy, philosophy, and living and dying and been involved in the production of numerous videos and films.

Probably the most widely recognised proposal from Yalom's work is the list of therapeutic factors, previously designated (in early editions) as 'curative factors'. These form the core of his model for group therapy:

> The therapeutic factors constitute the central organizing principle of this book . . . I . . . describe a psychotherapeutic approach based on these factors.
>
> (ibid., p. xii)

These factors are designated:

> Installation of hope; universality; imparting information; altruism; the corrective recapitulation of the primary family group; development of socializing techniques; imitative behaviour; interpersonal learning; group cohesiveness; catharsis; existential factors.
>
> (ibid., p. 1)

Yalom stipulates that these factors are inter-dependent; some are specifically mechanisms for change (e.g., socialising techniques), and others may serve as conditions for change (e.g., hope and cohesiveness).

Those who are at all familiar with the most fundamental tenets of existential philosophy and therapy will recognise that a few of these factors are not aligned with that philosophical psychotherapeutic model, e.g., the corrective recapitulation of the primary family group. However, there are also a number of factors that bear some relevance for existential thought and practice, e.g., universality (in terms of existential themes) and inter-personal learning (as related to inter-subjective understanding). These similarities, where they exist, will be clarified when the possible therapeutic effects of the existential paradigm are discussed.

Suffice it to note that 'existential factors' are the last on the list. Yalom notes:

> The category of existential factors was almost an afterthought.
>
> (ibid., p. 88)

The information reviewed so far is in reference to Yalom's book on the theory and practice of group psychotherapy, which was published initially in 1970. Yalom's text on existential psychotherapy, which probably rivals the former publication in notoriety, was issued in 1980; and has a distinctly different slant on the centrality of existential thought.

The therapeutic principle in the text on group psychotherapy, which is allotted a great deal of significance in the process described by Yalom, is that of inter-personal interaction, reflected in many of the factors delineated previously – in fact, he describes it as 'crucial' (ibid., p. xiv).

He goes on to state:

> The truly potent therapy group first provides an arena for patients to inter-act freely with others, then helps them to identify and understand what goes wrong in their interactions.
>
> (ibid., p. xiv)

This proposal is reminiscent of the emphasis on the inter-subjective nature of existence that is paramount in the existential model. However, there is a notable distinction in that the existential phenomenological asserts that existence is funda-mentally a 'with-world', not an assembly of distinct egos or entities; this peculiar-ity will be raised when the outline for the latter project is reviewed in more detail.

Yalom poses a linear chronological view of the therapeutic process, as well as of the therapeutic work:

> Chapters 8 through 14 present a chronological view of the therapy group . . . and the therapist's techniques that are relevant to each stage.
>
> (ibid., p. xvi)

Yalom's text follows a distinct line of group development, and therapist strate-gies and 'techniques' are referenced according to this progression. Some of these options for commentary will be reviewed with respect to the nature of 'dialogue' and the contributions of hermeneutics to an existential project.

This premise could appear to be a bit prescriptive. It will be suggested that group processes are more closely related to the qualities of the relationships among members (including the therapist). The case will be made that these relationships are constantly in flux and subject to ambivalence: the therapist is likely to tune into these variations as they occur and act accordingly, rather than to anticipate particular chronological stages.

Additionally, and most importantly, Yalom's philosophical view of time is clearly embedded in popular western thought: he emphasises the 'here and now' perspective for the work. He subscribes to the classic psychodynamic notions of 'transference', which is an assumption that disclaims the reality of the therapeutic (and other) relationship(s). He also includes a therapeutic factor that references a 'corrective recapitulation of the primary family group' (Yalom, 1995, p. 13). These principles place him firmly in the tradition of inside/outside dichotomy and demonstrate an allegiance to the notion of determinism.

There is a nod to the impact of nurture, in terms of early familial conditions; much like others proponents reviewed here, he places priority on the individual.

These perspectives are shared by most models of therapy, including the humanistic paradigms that claim affinity with existential thought (as in Yalom's subsequent text on the subject).

The themes of temporality and inter-subjectivity from an existential phenomenological view will be compared and contrasted with the more popular positions on these topics in Part II of this book.

However, there is a potent proposal, even as it is rooted in the 'here-and-now' principle, which resonates with an existential project: the discovery and creation of meaning.

Yalom delineates this two-tiered process:

> The first tier is the experiencing one: members live in the here-and-now . . . *immediate events in the meeting take precedence over events both in the current outside life and in the distant past of the members* . . . the second tier . . . is the *illumination of process* . . . the group . . . must transcend pure experience and apply itself to the integration of that experience.
>
> (ibid., p. 129–130, italics original)

Yalom purports that these two levels are necessary for a therapeutic effect. Tier one provides intensity and liveliness; tier two provides a deeper understanding of the meaning and significance of the experience. If the first event, the experience, is appreciated without the reflective follow-up, it will be a powerful but fleeting episode, with little recognition of the significance of the occurrence; if theorising or intellectualising takes priority over experience, the result will be much less potent and personal.

We may recall the revelation described by Lewin with reference to experiential learning, and also the emphasis in Foulkes' work on inter-personal learning.

The idea that we inevitably assign meaning to all our experiences is fundamental in existential phenomenological thought, as will be discussed in Chapters 16 and 21. The concept of time as linear, referenced in the 'here-and-now' emphasis, will be challenged when we consider alternate views on temporality, and the implications that this view holds for understanding the therapeutic process (and, indeed, life in general) will be clarified.

The possibilities for change are linked to the therapeutic factors listed earlier: *how* this happens takes up a major portion of Yalom's' text, and there seem to be innumerable overlaps and combinations of factors and effects.

However, there appear to be a few specific, readily identifiable therapeutic occurrences.

In his description of 'insight', Yalom offers:

> Patients may gain a more objective perspective on their *interpersonal presentation.*
>
> (ibid., p. 45, italics original)

It is hoped that when the patient discovers that their intentions to be experienced as a certain type of person fail, it is an opportunity to experiment, within the group (at least at first; then it may be tested 'outside'), with different behaviours that may produce more desirable results.

This insight may also lead to the recognition of the responsibility that the patient carries in 'creating' their relational world.

Additionally:

> Patients may learn *why* they do what they do with other people.
>
> (ibid., p. 45)

Thus, insight can take the form of *motivational* insight, which is a mechanism of change, *or genetic* insight, in which they also discover how their developmental history contributes to their behaviour.

In both cases, 'insight' is something that occurs 'inside' the individual, even though it is a consequence of (some kind) of inter-personal interaction. This supposition also indicates that Yalom subscribes to the inside/outside dichotomy.

Among the many discussions related to the nature of change, Yalom poses an interesting question:

> After all, the object of therapy is change, not self-understanding. Or is it? Or are the two synonymous? Or does any and every type of self-understanding lead automatically to change?
>
> (ibid., p. 83)

Yalom admits there is not a ready answer to this query; the notion of self-understanding itself warrants considerable thought and will be reviewed subsequently.

The idea of change, in Yalom's works, is often associated with the principle of 'responsibility'. Patients come to therapy most often looking for a 'change', and too often expect this to occur either without much effort on their part; or they arrive with demands and expectations that others should make changes that better accommodate their own wishes, or that would at least create a more favourable environment for the realisation of their own aims.

In commenting on the effective therapy group, Yalom notes:

> The interactional therapy group enhances responsibility assumption not only by making members aware of their personal contribution to their unsatisfying life situations but also by accentuating each member's role in the conduct of the group.
>
> (Yalom, 1980, p. 240)

This is a clear representation of how self-understanding might lead to change, and to what *kind* of change: that of becoming aware of how one's own choices contribute to one's situation, *by virtue of inter-personal learning*.

Yalom goes on to suggest that if and when members become aware of the part they play in the functioning, or dysfunction, of the group, they will also recognise that they have the power, as well as the 'obligation', to effect change in other life contexts.

How this is facilitated by both members and therapist has in part been elucidated previously, in the list of therapeutic factors. However, Yalom emphasises the power of one type of intervention that he claims is unique to the group setting: process commentary.

Process commentary, also sometimes known as 'mass commentary', is a summary referencing 'here and now' interactions (including non-verbal as well as verbal communications) among members; such an observation serves to grant some insight into the nature and quality of the inter-personal relationships of those present.

Yalom states that this strategy can be too risky for a group member to attempt, at least early on in the group development; it is often received as criticism, which could lead to a counter-attack, something likely to negatively affect group safety at an early stage. Additionally, group members bear the guilt or responsibility for the current situation and therefore cannot separate themselves from the context sufficiently enough to be objective.

This kind of observation will be further clarified when the review of a 'dialogical' attitude is described in some detail; it will be suggested that this can be a very useful communication in any relationship, including that of individual therapy, in which case it would refer to the dynamics between therapist and client.

Finally, it is important to note that Yalom states that '*it is the group that is the agent of change*' (Yalom, 1995, p. 109, italics original): this relegates the therapist to the position of participant/observer with some practical responsibilities that reside with them alone, such as the logistical aspects of time, place, and contractual issues. This is a view that shares some affinity with an existential model, and this description of the role of the therapist in groupwork is prevalent in many contemporary humanistic models.

## References

Yalom, I.D. *Existential Psychotherapy*, 1980, Basic Books, New York.
———. *The Theory and Practice of Group Psychotherapy*, 1995, Basic Books, New York.

# Chapter 7

# Conclusion and summary, Part I

We have seen how the divides titled nature/nurture and inside/outside, Cartesian in their essence, are and remain the basis for a popular view of human existence. The debate over which aspect, nature or nurture, takes precedence in the consideration of how we develop and 'become' still rages. The notions that the 'real person' is 'inside' and the 'self' is an entity quite separate from its environment are the foundation for most psychological, and many philosophical, models of subjective existence.

This begs the question as to how the subject is able to relate to, have knowledge of, and communicate with the outside, including others that are 'outside': we are left with an 'egocentric predicament' (Langdridge, 2007, p. 13).

These suppositions have inestimable import for the role of the therapist, the responsibilities of group members, and the aims of therapy.

Aligned with this perspective, psychoanalysis introduced a number of mechanisms by which a subject 'acted upon' the objects it encountered (including other people). Projection and transference, both means by which we impose our expectations and illusions onto another person, is probably the most well known of these activities. This view suggests, quite categorically, that the relationship between therapist and patient is fundamentally *unreal*, based as it is on illusion or delusion. Additionally, this process implies that the person so acted upon bears no responsibility, and is not in any way implicated, in the construction of the subject's experience: when applied to a fellow being, one might say that this principle can have a dehumanising effect.

These views are clearly represented in Bion's definitions of the three assumptions that impede the task of the work group. This supposition of the transferential nature of the therapist/patient relationship positions the therapist as the one who holds the 'correct' perspective on the patient's problems; thus, the therapist holds a great deal of power and is responsible for directing the therapeutic work.

The notion of transference also emphasises the importance of early experiences. The misconstrued events (relationships) of childhood are seen as the source of current difficulties and are addressed via transference interpretations. Yalom also shows a preference for this view in his list of therapeutic factors, particularly the factor designated 'the corrective recapitulation of the primary family group' (Yalom, 1995, p. 24), which is achieved via such interventions.

This notion of determinism, even when mitigated by a 'here-and-now' focus, presents a clear affinity for a very linear view of time. This supposition will be challenged when we consider the existential phenomenological perspective and the implications thereof for the work.

The dichotomy of inside/outside also gave rise to the concepts of the conscious and unconscious aspects of the mind, forever separated by an impenetrable barrier (except for the application of psychoanalysis). The unconscious harboured impulses and desires that were unacceptable in extremis; this was the 'nature' element of our psychic composition, mitigated with some little success by our conscious ego, which represented the influence of 'nurture' that stood guard at the gateway of the libidinous torrent.

This assertion then requires a 'divination' of unconscious material, as it represents the repressed elements of thought and experience, an endeavour that must be led by a skilled professional; again, the therapist is at the helm. In this approach, conscious content is subordinated: the message is that 'things are not as they seem' (even, or especially, to the patient).

Lewin, Bion, and Foulkes were working contemporaneously. Bion was the pioneer that adhered most closely to psychodynamic tenets as applied to groupwork; Lewin and Foulkes – the former a social psychologist, the latter a trained analyst and psychiatrist – were both influenced by Gestalt psychology, and these studies informed their perspective on the inter-relational quality of human existence, as well as the significance of inter-relational experiential learning (although it has been noted that Foulkes exhibited an ambivalence towards classic psychodynamic theory; see Cohn, 1997; Dalal, 1998).

Rogers, a more contemporary theorist and practitioner, displays a deep appreciation of some of the inter-relational emphases that were recognised, in some form, by Lewin and Foulkes. The relationships between therapist and group members in the person-centered model were decidedly egalitarian. This allowed the therapist to participate as a 'genuine' person and did not require some superior or specialised theoretical insight into the nature of being human: the therapist was one among many.

In his book on group psychotherapy (1995), Yalom displayed a mixture of views that encompassed both psychodynamic and 'humanistic' elements. He stated that the group was the agent of change, but also aligned himself with notions of the unconscious and of transference. Ultimately, for Yalom, it was the unconscious material that took precedence over conscious behaviour. Yalom gave a great deal of credit to the inter-relational aspects of the learning experience, but these were appreciated only as the backdrop for the recapitulations of earlier relationships. In short, Yalom displays some ambiguity with reference to a number of issues, including the use of the past.

In the model proposed by Yalom, the responsibility for transference interpretations, as well as process commentary, lies primarily with the therapist, although the group is implicated in sharing the burden of the work. In Bion's model, the therapist is (supposedly) privileged with insight as to the nature of the transferences and therefore holds an informed view of the process. In Lewin's work, the group is primarily responsible for their own learning (although one must bear in mind that Lewin wasn't intent on producing a paradigm for therapy). In Roger's work, we see the most dramatic examples of an egalitarian stance and laissez faire attitude among all the practitioners.

In sum, of the four pioneers reviewed, it would appear that Kurt Lewin, in his field theory and his appreciation of the Gestalt notion of figure/ground as it represents human belonging, and S. H. Foulkes, in his assertion that 'each individual is ... basically and centrally determined ... by the world in which he lives' (Foulkes, 1983, p. 10), are the two theorists most closely aligned with the existential phenomenological perspective on inter-subjectivity. This parallel will be further illuminated in the Parts II and III of this book.

Lewin's description of the psychological field, or 'lifespace' (Lewin, 1948) – which is comprised of the person and their group(s) as the fundamental factor in the consideration of behaviour – is the most adamant and unambiguous declaration of the primacy of the group. It is within this plexus of human co-existence that 'change' takes place; it is within this network that we source our very identities, and our fates.

# References

Cohn, H. *Existential Thought and Therapeutic Practice*, 1997, Sage Publications, London.

Dalal, F. *Taking the Group Seriously*, 1998, Jessica Kingsley Publishers, London.

Foulkes, S.H. *Introduction to Group-Analytic Psychotherapy*, 1983, Karnac, London.

Langdridge, D. *Phenomenological Psychology, Theory, Research and Method*, 2007, Pearson Education Ltd., Harlow, England.

Lewin, K. *Resolving Social Conflict*, 1948 (ed. G. Lewin), Harper and Brothers Publishers, New York.

Yalom, I. *Existential Psychotherapy*, 1980, Basic Books, New York.

———. *The Theory and Practice of Group Psychotherapy*, 1995, Basic Books, New York.

# Part II

# Being and doing

# Chapter 8

# Towards an existential phenomenological model for group psychotherapy and counselling

There are distinguishing principles of the existential phenomenological paradigm that would seem to make it particularly relevant to the group psychotherapeutic project, but before we proceed, it is probably wise to issue a caveat about the proposals that will be presented.

No theory about psychotherapy can provide definitive strategies for the practitioner; no philosophy of the human condition will ever provide all the answers. It can be appreciated, then, that there will always be a 'gap' in our understanding about what is happening in any given relationship or situation.

The limits inherent in all understanding will be considered further, and the basis for this assertion will be shown to apply generally to notions of 'truth' and to human existence in general.

In his book *How to Do Groups*, Friedman suggests that every psychotherapeutic theory explains what is happening, what might happen, and what to pay attention to, as well as how to engage with these manifestations; these are commonly referred to as *procedural issues* (Friedman, 1994). He goes on to discuss a variety of techniques common among humanistic traditions.

The problem arises when the therapist or, indeed, other group members encounter an event or behaviour that seemingly does not 'fit' with the adopted theory. There can be a temptation to construe this occurrence in a manner that *enforces* alignment with the model. The ethical, therapeutic, and practical hazards of such an endeavour are probably apparent.

If the practitioner does not satisfactorily succeed in this 'refit', we recognise that this may leave them in a position of 'not knowing', a position which may appear to be a fault. In the following discussion, we will begin to appreciate that this is exactly the status to which the existential phenomenological therapist *aspires*.

The warning issued, then, is that the philosophical model does not lend itself readily to 'technique'; it is a process of exploration and unfolding that can be viewed more as an art than a science.

Based as it is in philosophy, the existential phenomenological model provides some understanding of the human predicament (as do all psychological and philosophical schools) and supports psychotherapeutic practice with a method grounded in an *attitude*. This phenomenological attitude and the correlated method will be covered subsequently in greater detail.

However, the point posited here is that the 'doing' of therapy is grounded in the 'being' or, perhaps even more appropriately, the 'being-with' of those involved. Hence, this book is structured to introduce those 'being-with' conditions that may provide the foundation for 'doing-with'.

This approach requires a great deal of a practitioner: vulnerability, accessibility, the capacity for un-knowing and staying with it, the willingness to encounter the Other and, sometimes, 'failure' in being present in the way we might wish to be. As an experiment in being-with, therapy grants no objectivity or authority to the therapist: one must expect the unexpected.

Within the various strands of existential thinking, there are a few basic proposals shared by philosophical sources, and there are also a number of divergences. In an attempt at an inclusive description of the tradition, Macquarrie calls it a 'style of philosophizing' (Macquarrie, 1973, p. 14).

Rollo May elaborates further on how philosophy informs practice:

> Existentialism is not a system of therapy but an attitude toward therapy.
>
> (May, 1969, p. 15)

The most widely recognised common premise among proponents of this approach is probably that any consideration of what it means to be human must begin with the existing person, the subject as they are becoming, emerging. This is related to the origins of the word 'existence', which is rooted in a Latin verb indicating 'standing out' or 'to move out'.

Macquarrie adds to this:

> The verb had a more active *feel* about it. . . . Putting it more philosophically, to exist is to stand out from nothing.
>
> (Macquarrie, 1973, p. 62, italics original)

As to the focus of the philosophical project, Friedman makes this assertion:

> the actual situation of the existential subject as the starting point of thought.
>
> (Friedman, 1992, p. 4)

Human existence can only be understood via reflection on what it means 'to be'. Humans are the beings who concern themselves with this inquiry; in fact, how one lives one's life is the response to the question.

In providing something of a representation of the notion of 'becoming', we might note that this is a process, one that lasts a lifetime, and that it is difficult, if not impossible (as the existentialist would claim), to assign an 'essence' to something that is dynamic. We are very different from, for example, a rock, which is defined by its essential composition.

Jean Paul Sartre's postulate that 'existence precedes essence' is a succinct pronouncement of this view (Sartre, 1958). This is an assertion referring to the concept of 'self': it disputes the notion that there exists a 'core' self or an 'intra-psychic' or 'internal' entity that is compartmentalised. More will be made of this argument in the following discussions.

Hence, we arrive at another fundamental tenet, that 'becoming' with respect to human beings is realised in choice, and where there's choice there's freedom, and where there's freedom there is responsibility.

Additionally, where there is freedom there is meaning and value demonstrated in our choices, and there is 'death' in the form of the options we abandon. In engaging with choice and freedom, we suffer angst as we wrestle with the uncertainty of making the 'right' choice (only to re-evaluate it later as the not-so-right choice, thereby reinforcing uncertainty). We are affected in our bodies by the anxiety surrounding these deliberations, as well as by the dismay or jubilation about consequences of the option chosen that were *not* foreseen. We reach for language that will allow us to share these struggles, in the hope of feeling not quite so alone, and in this regard we need and want others (or sometimes not). We know that we do not have all the time in the world – death puts an end to all human endeavours. We recognise *that* it will happen, but not where or when (this holds true even for cases of suicide, as we have heard from recounts of unsuccessful attempts).

And we experience all this in the midst of others, a matrix of subjects like ourselves, and whose very presence has an ineluctable impact on every aspect of our being and becoming.

It is this notion of the 'field' of relatedness, this appreciation of the plexus composed of nodal points of other existents, the principles of inclusion and mutuality demonstrated in the design of the Taijitu of Yin and Yang (neither which would 'be' without the other), that makes existential phenomenological precepts a sound basis for a model of therapeutic groupwork.

DuBose puts it this way:

> the . . . jambalaya, where the very Andouille sausage takes on its 'is-ness', and gets its 'this-ness' ONLY in relation to the other ingredients and vice versa. . . . You can take any one of those ingredients out of the dish and it is something different, but there is no 'out' of context. If I take the jambalaya rice out . . . its is-ness is still in some other context, such as . . . a staple of survival. . . . The point is that rice is what it is in relation to anything/everything else.
>
> (DuBose, cited in Spinelli, 2016)

There we have a delicious metaphor for the inter-relatedness of human existence, which encompasses not just other people, but everything that *is*.

## References

Friedman, M. *The Worlds of Existentialism: A Critical Reader*, 1992, Humanities Press International, Atlantic Highlands, NJ, and London, UK.
Friedman, W.H. *How to Do Groups*, 1994, Jason Aronson Inc, New York.
Macquarrie, J. *Existentialism*, 1973, Penguin Books, London.
May, R. (ed.). *Existential Psychology*, 1969, McGraw Hill, New York.
Sartre, J.P. *Being and Nothingness*, 1958 (trans. H. Barnes), Routledge, London.
Spinelli, E. 'Relatedness: Contextualising Being and Doing in Existential Therapy', 2016, *Journal of the Society for Existential Analysis*, vol. 27.2, p. 323.

# Chapter 9

# Why group

As has been suggested previously, human existence is fundamentally inter-subjective and inter-relational. Heidegger situates 'Dasein', his word for the human being (etymologically, it means 'being-there'; Polt, 1999, p. 28), in a 'with-world' (Heidegger, 1962).

The 'with-world' includes objects as well as people, and human perspectives on these phenomena are in part a by-product of their *involvement* in their situation. This implies the impossibility of absolute objectivity, as we cannot have a 'God's-eye' view of our situation.

All the concerns of humans, all the beliefs, hopes, desires, and assumptions, are not 'inside' one's head: they are in-relation-to-the-world, to a world-with others.

If, for example, we harbour a belief about an issue, it is directed towards something (or someone) in the world. Even if we take our self, or a 'psychic object' (like a thought), as the focus of our attention, it is, obviously, in the world, as it is I who is 'there'.

Merleau-Ponty, colleague of Jean Paul Sartre, offered further clarification:

> There is no inner man: man is in the world and only in the world does he know himself.
>
> (Merleau-Ponty, 1962, p. xi)

This immersion in the world will be elucidated when we look at phenomenology and how this contributes to how we 'know' ourselves, and others, or indeed, what is meant by 'knowing', in a phenomenological sense.

With reference to the shared aspect of existence, Cohn asserts:

> Relatedness is a primary state of being – we cannot choose a world without other people.
>
> (Cohn, 1997, p. 13)

Even when we seek to be apart from others, the very concept of 'apartness' implies relationship: we may achieve some distance, but this is still within the inter-subjective context.

It is likely clear that this condition of human existence is the most compelling recommendation for group psychotherapy: we are always and concurrently participants in many groups.

This principle is espoused in the work of Foulkes, who emphasised the interrelatedness of life in his notion of the 'matrix' (which was informed by the Gestalt theory of figure/ground configuration of experience) and went so far as to claim that

> It would be true to say that group psychotherapy is indicated whenever psychotherapy is indicated.
>
> (Foulkes, 1986, p. 65)

The foremost aim and hope of group therapy is that members will have the opportunity to hear about, recognise, and explore, in situ, the effects they have on others. This was demonstrated in the Northfield experiment in which Foulkes was involved, and which was reviewed in a previous chapter (Chapter 4, S.H. Foulkes).

The result of 'feedback 'from group constituents allows for 'experiential' learning. This kind of situation provides powerful, if sometimes disturbing, information on how one's strategies for and hopes of being experienced as a person with particular attributes, of being perceived in certain ways, is successful, at all or in part.

This kind of revelation may well challenge one to reconsider one's behaviour: some experimentation may ensue, followed by further feedback and reports. The revisions may continue indefinitely, but this exchange demonstrates how our 'identities' are forged in the 'in-between'.

Cohn reflects on this dynamic:

> the 'individual' is indeed an abstraction . . . and can only be understood in a context of mutual disclosures . . . what we see as psychological disturbances are then disturbances in this context, disturbances of relatedness and communication.
>
> (Cohn, 1997, p. 55)

The aim of group therapy, then, is to clarify these disturbances. The therapist may assist in this process – their role is generally seen as that of an 'enabler' – but the group is equally responsible for the work.

This notion of who and how we are 'being' as a result of interaction is mooted by many philosophical and psychological sources. Sartre comments:

> The Other *looks* at me and as such holds the secret of my being, he knows what I *am*.
>
> (Sartre, 1969, p. 363, italics original)

This maxim suggests that others are free to interpret one as they wish. In that moment, it is 'true', as it is the perception of the one who looks, However, one is not 'totalised' by an single episode, as the other may change their appraisal. We also have evidence that others in our social world may experience us differently from any current contact.

It is no wonder, then, that we are anxious, and wary, of relationships. We seek to find confidence in the Other; we hope to build trust in an effort to keep ourselves safe from the 'look' that 'fixes' us in a manner we lament. When the look awards the confirmation we seek, we are aware, even then, that it could be withdrawn. However, we are capable of reciprocation, as we choose, and therein resides our power.

Perhaps we recognise in this exchange the basis for Sartre's axiom that 'hell is – other people' (Sartre, 1955, p. 47).

The group context facilitates an appreciation of how we each contribute to the *self-other* construct, as described. Group members may recognise that the experience of the group itself – the interactional network – rather than just the topics discussed, provides the information that can enlighten us as to how we are experienced and how this view accords with or diverges from how we aspire to be with others.

Finally, it is important to note that there is an obvious difference from, and advantage to, the group therapy format as opposed to that of individual therapy, that is, the inter-relational *complexity* of the situation. Engagement with a multiplicity of world-views, intentions, strategies, and desires can be every bit as challenging as those we encounter in our wider communities and contacts.

Spinelli comments:

> The therapy world of existential group psychotherapy provides a structure that is more akin to each group member's wider world relations than any one-to-one form of therapy could ever hope to be.
>
> (Spinelli, 2007, p. 204)

In sum, we are inevitably constituents of groups, in the plural. Sometimes these are groups that we willingly choose, to which we gladly subscribe. Others are groups to which we are 'assigned', in which case we are regarded as a member of a group that may not align with our values, or to which we hold no allegiance, but, as in the situation described in the 'the look' vignette, we are consigned to these networks by someone else's perspective of or opinion about us.

We are subject to one another's description of who and how we are, although such a perspective cannot be the total, complete, or final definition. In the group therapeutic endeavour, these issues can be recognised, and engaged with, which can lead to more fulfilling and productive ways of being with others.

# References

Cohn, H.W. *Existential Thought and Therapeutic Practice*, 1997, Sage Publications, London.

Foulkes, S.H. *Group Analytic Psychotherapy*, 1986, Karnac, London.

Heidegger, M. *Being and Time*, 1962 (trans. J. Macquarrie), Blackwell, Oxford, UK.

Merleau-Ponty, M. *Phenomenology of Perception*, 1962 (trans. C. Smith), Routledge, London.

Polt, R. *Heidegger, an Introduction*, 1999, UCL Press Ltd., London.

Sartre, J.P. *No Exit and Three Other Plays*, 1955 (trans. G. Stuart), Vintage Books, New York, NY.

Sartre, J.P. *Being and Nothingness*, 1969 (trans. H. Barnes), Routledge, London.

Spinelli, E. *Practicing Existential Psychotherapy*, 2007, Sage Publications, London.

# Chapter 10

# The existential givens of human existence

The conditions of human existence in existential literature are referred to as 'onto-logical' categories, and the particular manner in which any one of us responds to or engages with these givens is known as 'ontic'.

As has been suggested previously, the existential thinker begins with what is *so* for any being: *what i*s being experienced, and *how* it is being experienced.

Iacovou and Weixel-Dixon note:

> As human beings we are both ontic (we are entities that exist) and ontological (we are able to ask questions about our existence, to consider possibilities).
>
> (Iacovou and Weixel-Dixon, 2015, p. 23)

The universal concerns for all human beings are 'those intrinsic aspects of being that are . . . unescapable' (Cohn, 1997, p. 12). As such, they are common to every culture, every era, and every person: these shared concerns afford a place to begin to understand each other, and ourselves, and offer a perspective on what it means to be human.

This perspective might be seen as a context for both diversity and affinity: we are all the same, and different.

This theory of human existence is what *informs* the practitioner. It is the basis for the practical endeavour of therapeutic engagement; the *how* of existential practice is an extension of the understanding of the human predicament (Weixel-Dixon, 2017).

Gordon Allport, in a text edited by Rollo May, supports this principle of the relationship between theory and practice:

> *Existentialism deepens the concepts that define the human condition.* In so doing, it prepares the way (for the first time) for a *psychology of mankind.*
>
> (Allport, in May, 1969, p. 94, italics original)

As has been proposed, we exist in a 'with-world'. It is imperative to appreciate that these conditions are engaged with by a person who exists in an inter-related field; our experiences are in the world and our responses to these givens have import for, and impact upon, our inter-subjective situation.

What follows is a list of themes that reflect the shared concerns of human existence. Each will be considered for their relevance to group psychotherapy and counselling. These are themes of which we are aware, as beings and practitioners, and to which we are sensitive, as we attend to ourselves and our clients.

In being aware of these themes, we hope to offer the opportunity to enter into explorations of how we engage with, or avoid and deny, these issues. The existential therapist argues that such denial of these sometimes disturbing and challenging aspects of life produces problems: these aspects cannot, will not, be denied without negative, if not dire, consequences. Thus, we must find ways to meet them that will enhance our existence instead of impoverishing it.

For example: a common denial of the issue of death might be refusal to take appropriate measures to prepare for the ultimate event by considering final arrangements, or to clarify wishes in the event of incapacitation; or, to operate on the assumption that one has unlimited time for all those projects that we neglect, avoid, or never complete.

The attitude and method of these explorations will be outlined in the review of phenomenology, but we had a preview of some of those principles when we alluded to the exploration of *what* we experience and *how* we experience it.

It was proposed earlier that we have at least some limited capacity for choice and freedom. These are exercised in how we respond to these givens; how we *live* our attitudes towards these intrinsic qualities frames our very existence.

All givens are inter-related: it is nearly impossible to speak of one without implicating another. Where this overlap is particularly obvious, it will be noted in the discussion.

This list is the view of this author; there are many variations on these elements.

As the discussion outlines these conditions, there will be examples given of how these might manifest in group communications in terms of verbal and behavioural contributions. These particulars are the product of many years of groupwork experience; there will be many more that are not specified. In fact, the possible responses are really innumerable.

## References

Allport, G. 'Comment on Earlier Chapters', in *Existential Psychology*, 1969 (ed. R. May) (second ed.), McGraw Hill, Inc., New York, NY.

Cohn, H.W. *Existential Thought and Therapeutic Practice*, 1997, Sage, London.

Iacovou, S., and Weixel-Dixon, K. *Existential Therapy, Key Points and Techniques*, 2015, Routledge, Abingdon, UK, and New York.

Weixel-Dixon, K. *Interpersonal Conflict, an Existential, Psychotherapeutic and Practical Model*, 2017, Routledge, London.

# Chapter 11

# Time and temporality

We begin with a consideration of time, known in the philosophical literature as temporality. This latter term refers to how humans experience time, as opposed to simply a means of measuring this phenomenon.

Time is most often delineated by three precise dimensions: the past, the present, and the future.

However, this common view of time is challenged in much of the existential philosophical literature, and this has certainly informed the practice of existential psychotherapy. The work of Martin Heidegger as well as that of M. Merleau-Ponty, provides a dramatic starting point to this discussion. Merleau-Ponty asserts:

> Each moment of time calls all the others to witness.
>
> (Merleau-Ponty, 1962, p. 69)

This suggests that a reference to any one of the temporal dimensions *implicates* the others. When we speak of the past, we stand in the present as we recall a former occasion. We often review the past in an effort to guide us in making choices that will affect our future. We constantly seek to discern the 'best' option, one that will produce the future as we wish and hope it to be.

Thus, it is postulated that the three dimensions of time, in terms of any human concern, are concurrent and *convergent* rather than consecutive.

The very notion of choice implies a striving to direct *change*. This may be change that is forced upon us, or a change that we fear or anticipate, or change intended to create a situation that will best accommodate our intentions for ourselves and others.

As discussed previously, this idea that we struggle to make a choice or to actualise an option that will bring into effect the circumstances to which we aspire is the source of a great deal of anxiety (this anxiety will be revisited in a later topic). This illustrates that we strive for the 'not-yet'.

By virtue of these tenets, it would seem that it is the *future* that is favoured as the most significant dimension. Martin Heidegger supports this position in his description of the human existent as 'being-towards-death' (Heidegger, 1962). Our death is the only event of which we can be certain: it is the ultimate boundary, it is a possibility (at any given moment), and this eventuality (inevitably) inclines us to the future. Until that very final moment, we are in the process of becoming: we are incomplete and never really coincide with ourselves as a 'finished' project.

Heidegger's seminal work, *Being and Time* (1962), puts temporality at the centre of the consideration of what it means to be human. He states quite categorically:

> Time must be . . . genuinely conceived as the horizon for all understanding of Being and for any way of interpreting it.
>
> (Heidegger, 1962, p. 39)

This understanding becomes more apparent as we examine the effects of temporality further.

Previously, it was proposed that human existence is both ontic, as in we 'exist', and ontological, in that we as humans can question the nature and basis for our existence. This kind of inquiry produces responses as to how and why we exist; it also indicates that we *care* about these issues.

'Care', or 'concern', is reflected in our questions of 'what is the meaning of life' and 'what is the purpose of *my* life'. These questions would lose much of their import and impetus if we had all the time necessary to choose and re-choose infinitely; we could always avail ourselves of another opportunity to 'correct' our choices. However, it is clear that as our time is limited, and in ways unpredictable, choosing becomes anxiety laden.

The future pulls us towards the creation of purpose and to actualising options that will satisfy, to some extent, the meanings and values we assign to our lives. The past serves, to some degree, as a 'boundary' to our freedom to choose specific options.

The options available to us at any given time are grounded in the two contexts: one is that over which we have no control, and the other is the consequence of previous choices.

Where and when we were born, to whom we were born, our racial origins, and the various other practical elements of our life, for each of us in particular, are elements beyond our control, We are 'thrown' into existence, this existence that I identify as mine, specifically, and that could have all been otherwise; this is the source of contingency, in that there is no 'reason' for it.

Additionally, we are thrown into an existence that has 'givens', as reviewed in these chapters. We cannot choose to be in a world without others; we cannot choose immortality in a human form, etc.

This first category described is known as 'facticity': the unchosen basis of our existence with which we must contend.

The second category is that in which we exercise, and have exercised, our agency within certain parameters.

Our limitations in terms of our options, as related to the past, are grounded in the choices we have made previously. I have, in actualising some options and abandoning others, circumscribed my current possibilities. For example, if a person chooses to have their reproductive organs sterilised, at a point in their lives where this seems to be the 'right' decision, their options in terms of becoming a parent will be radically minimised, if not eradicated. Or, if someone chooses to do a four-year degree in a particular subject and then decides to pursue another profession, those four years cannot be recouped, and this factor may impose limitations on their current opportunities.

From these principles, we can appreciate that past events are not viewed as determinants of our current situation: it is our *current attitude* towards previous experiences that informs our immediate perspective and choices.

It is also apparent that we can and do change our evaluations of past incidents with reference to current perspectives. An example of this would be a past relationship that was brought to an end and, at the time, seemed earth shattering; from a current view, it might appear that this curtailed romance seems to be the better outcome. The inverse is also possible: we can reconsider a previous 'mistaken' choice as one that now feels appropriate, with respect to current circumstances. Of course, these re-evaluations can continue indefinitely.

Finally, the past cannot be repeated: we are never in exactly the same situation, as time has passed and we, and the world, have moved with it.

Boss notes this principle:

> For someone who is mortal, no situation happens twice in quite the same way. If what he does is not in tune with the moment, that moment is irrevocably lost to him.
>
> (Boss, 1994, p. 121)

It is often suggested that group psychotherapy should focus on the 'here and now'. Apart from this condition being extremely elusive, there is no rationale for demanding a temporal focus. The three dimensions are referenced in relation to each other; any one is ripe for exploration, and such an enquiry will have repercussions for perspectives on the past, present, and future, contemporaneously.

## Examples of how this theme may be manifested in practice

The duration of the session is an obvious consideration in terms of the time element: the therapist will have some rationale for this aspect, but it must be clear to all involved what is expected with reference to promptness and attendance. When these contractual aspects are breached, it should be noted that all parties are affected, and there is likely to be some communication as to *how* people are affected.

Therapist and group members share the responsibility for starting and ending the session in a timely manner: where this is not happening, it can be offered as a topic for reflection. If the group habitually adjourns noticeably early or late, this is noteworthy and can be a subject for discussion.

Likewise, the number of meetings will be introduced before the group meets: this topic, though contractual in nature, is always up for discussion. If there are a set number of meetings agreed, two common attitudes that result are: 'this is a very short time, so I won't invest much' (demotivation) or 'this is a very short time, so I must get as much out of it as possible' (possibly over-ambitious). Such attitudes have implications for how one lives, how one relates (how it matters to other members), and how one views death (to be considered further).

If the group is framed as an 'open' group, with members leaving and new members arriving, there may be considerable time 'spent' on reviewing past events or themes from the group's history, the purpose and effect of which can be reflected upon by all. There may be some mourning, or celebration, of the loss of members, as well as discussion about what it means to be a 'new' or an 'old' member.

At some point, the therapist is likely to offer a general observation (meta-commentary) on how the group uses the time: this is useful in episodes of 'stuckness', or of high emotion, when communication may be stifled or ineffective.

Members may have a proclivity for focusing, or insisting, on one dimension of time as the arena of discussion. This should be verbally noted by the therapist and offered to the group for exploration.

In groups that have at least one member who is habitually less talkative than the others, or else very much more verbal than others, it seems to be a common strategy – originating from the membership itself (and hopefully not from the therapist, who should not be dismayed by such disparities) – to suggest the use of a clock. This is meant to 'regulate' the duration of members' communications; such a demand generally produces a very fruitful exchange about the hopes, fears, and expectations harboured by the group members as to the nature of relatedness, communication, and trust. This is, of course, an important aspect of the work to be done.

## References

Boss, M. *Existential Foundations of Medicine and Psychology*, 1994 (trans. S. Conway and A. Cleaves), Jason Aronson, Northvale, NJ.

Heidegger, M. *Being and Time*, 1962 (trans. J. Macquarrie and E.H. Freund), Blackwell, UK.

Merleau-Ponty, M. *The Phenomenology of Perception*, 1962 (trans. C. Smith), Routledge and Kegan Paul, London.

# Chapter 12

# Relatedness

Much has already been said regarding the inter-subjective quality of human existence; there will be further considerations of this topic when we review the contributions of phenomenology.

The inter-subjective condition has been broached as a principal rationale and justification for the practice of group therapy and counselling; it seems to approximate more closely the multiplicity and complexity of relationships in our lives, and these similarities (and discrepancies) can be useful and informative.

However, each group will also provide new and distinct challenges from those we encounter in our relationships external to the therapy situation. The group cannot be a 'microcosm' of any other sets of relationships. For such a situation to occur, it would demand exact replicas of experiences, encounters, and persons; such occurrences are deemed impossible by virtue of the condition of temporality (see Chapter 11), and the process-like condition of self-and-other.

It would be a predictable with-world if we were objects, rather than subjects. If we were consistent entities readily identifiable by their static compositions, and the use we make of them, the uncertainty of being-with-others would be mitigated.

The attitude described is, in fact, identified by Sartre as an article of 'Bad Faith' (Sartre, 1969). We wish for others to be objects:

> We wish people to conform to the descriptions we give of them . . . we wish to predict their behaviour entirely. . . . Our reason for wishing this (is) . . . other people are essentially, in themselves, and by their very existence, a danger to us.
>
> (Warnock, 1970, p. 117)

What makes this an act of Bad Faith is that we 'objectify' the Other; we try to ignore that they have agency as we ourselves do in the hopes of denying them their freedom to objectify *oneself*. When we understand that we are being objectified, indeed, reified, we are being seen in some impoverished form.

Additionally, if I can maintain the illusion that the Other is *not* a free agent, then he can be identified as a character that will behave in predictable and specific ways – no surprises. 'He is only a waiter', as in the well-known example given by Sartre (1969).

We can note that this references uncertainty, another given of existence, and one that was briefly alluded to in an earlier section (Part II, Chapter 13, Uncertainty, angst, and anxiety).

I return to Jean Paul Sartre, and his descriptions of being with each other, to illuminate the impact we have on each other in terms of who and how we are.

In his story about the 'look', Sartre describes a man looking though a keyhole, spying on his lover; it is with some shock that he realises he too is being watched, and judged, perhaps characterised as a pervert. In that moment, he is an object for the one who looks at him, an entity of limited possibilities, and his freedom to define himself is minimised (Sartre, 1969).

Sartre puts it succinctly:

> Beyond any knowledge which I can have, I am this self which another knows. . . . We are dealing with my being as it is written in and by the Other's freedom.
>
> (Sartre, 1969, pp. 261–262)

However, as proposed previously, we are not totalised: not by any single 'look' of an Other, not by any single event or choice, or even for and by ourselves; our identity is realised in many episodes and remains an unfinished process until our death.

There are as many ways of being-with-others as there are meetings, but there is a particularly relevant description of a *mode* of relatedness for the project of psychotherapy: the quality of 'solicitude'.

As has been suggested previously, human beings 'care' about our existence. We also care about each other, but in a slightly different manner, that is, in 'solicitude', in Martin Heidegger's (1993) terms.

It can be understood that we are able to interact with other people in ways different from how we 'use' objects (although as posited, we sometimes seek to make objects of others). We can *participate* with other people; this is a principle, and a possibility, that we will study again, but suffice it to note here that we can influence, affect, and 'move' people with respect to how we are 'with' them, and these conditions can be reciprocal, beneficial, and/or mutual, or *not*.

Heidegger differentiates between an 'authentic' way of being-with and a less helpful way of engaging with another. In the first instance, we 'leap ahead' of the Other, in a sense, inviting them to find their way forward in a manner that is a result of their own choice and an actualisation of their own values. The other manner in which we engage is to 'leap in' for the Other, taking over *for* and *from* them, essentially taking over the work that belongs to them.

Cohn applies these distinctions to models of therapy:

> These two modes of solicitude are illustrated by two kinds of therapies – those that support clients by advice or medication, and those that help them understand their situation and their part in it.
>
> (Cohn, 2002, p. 38)

The second practice described would be the closer approximation of an authentic engagement.

The preferred engagement is considered authentic in that it seeks to challenge the client to be aware of their possibilities, their limitations, and the responsibility of choosing; the 'deficient' (Heidegger, 1993) mode of relatedness relegates these factors.

We can imagine that the authentic way of being with others as described here, and the good faith acknowledgement that others are free agents like ourselves, has implications for how we are as therapists, as well as how we are as constituents of the wider relational matrix of our lives.

Cohn emphasises:

> Any . . . opening up towards all that is and addresses us, is, in Heidegger's view, at the core of human existence, and a Being-with that helps to make this possible for the Other is an affirmation of Being-in-the-world.
>
> (Cohn, 2002, p. 38)

The import of this attitude is that it underpins the purpose of existential therapy, and indeed of life itself: to acknowledge and engage with the challenges, burdens, and blessings that constitute the fabric of human existence.

## Some examples of how this theme may be manifested in practice

To begin with, the proposal that we are all subject to the same concerns and issues creates a foundation of equality and cohesion: we are all in this together.

Thus it should come as no surprise that the therapist's participation is, for the most part, much the same as any other member of the group, apart from the responsibility of logistical arrangements. The therapist has the same latitude in terms of the nature of their contributions and shares the same struggles with vulnerability, exposure, and safety: all members are participants and observers.

It also follows that every member is responsible, to some degree, for the quality of the group communications. It is hoped, through feedback (more description of this process will come later), that they will come to recognise in what ways they contribute to this aspect.

Members will talk about relationships external to the group, as well as those within the therapy group: this is all relevant material. Comparisons between how we are with people in our wider inter-personal context and the co-members can yield a deeper understanding of our expectations of ourselves and others.

If members other than the therapist propose exercises, or 'behavioural experiments', it can be useful to consider the purpose of these, with reference to how relationships are developing and/or maintained. An example might be that one member proposes that group members role play significant figures from a particular member's past, an exercise most often associated with Gestalt therapy. Such a suggestion needn't be discouraged by the therapist, but it is most effective if the negotiations around this suggestion are allowed to run a natural course and are discussed until some consensus is reached; this decision may be revised or reconsidered.

Reflection on such an episode can yield significant communication and discoveries about privacy, disclosure, and candour: when it is 'safe' to be transparent, and when and why it feels a wiser course to withhold.

Conflict among members, and including the therapist, are to be expected; high emotions indicate an emotional investment in the situation. More will be offered in a separate section (part III, Chapter 31) on this phenomenon.

The inter-personal relationships among the group are as important as the narratives presented. These 'process issues' (*what* is happening) warrant as much attention as verbal communications; observations known as 'meta-commentary' can be offered by anyone in the group. The effects of such an interpretation will be considered subsequently in Chapter 24, Relational issues.

## References

Cohn, H.W. *Heidegger and the Roots of Existential Therapy*, 2002, Continuum, New York, NY.

Heidegger, M. *Being and Time*, 1993 (trans. J. Macquarrie and E. Robinson), Blackwell, Oxford.

Warnock, M. 1970, Oxford University Press, Oxford.

Warnock, M., *Existentialism*, 1992, Oxford University Press, Oxford.

Sartre, J.P. *Being and Nothingness*, 1969 (trans. H. Barnes), Routledge, Abingdon, UK.

# Chapter 13

# Uncertainty, angst, and anxiety

We are thrown into the world; the circumstances of our origins are contingent; and death looms as both a possibility (at any time) and an eventuality.

We become aware rather quickly that we cannot always bend others to our wishes and that the results of our efforts often yield unexpected results not only for ourselves but also for others. The same can be said of our concerted strategies to implement changes that produce specific results.

What can we be certain of? Only that, at times, we will be caught up in this condition.

Spinelli makes the point that

Uncertainty is a certainty of existence.

(Spinelli, 2007, p. 24)

This issue of uncertainty, as with other givens of existence, is an ontological condition: inevitable and unavoidable. How we respond to it is an ontic aspect, and it gives shape to our lives.

The emotional, that is, ontic, encounter with uncertainty produces anxiety. Anxiety is recognition of what troubles us, what threatens us. It may be a consequence of a pending or possible loss or the anticipation of the outcome of a given action or decision; it always references a specific fear. In this case, we may resort to strategies to manage, if not abolish, these identifiable fears.

A strict enforcement of such strategies can result in a 'closing down' of one's openness to the vagaries of existence, and it comes with some cost: we become blind to possibilities and struggle to remain 'static'.

As opposed to anxiety, which is an 'ontic', emotional experience, i.e., an experience that is primarily is relative to an individual, the term 'angst' is a reference to the ontological property of uncertainty: also undeniable (it is sometimes noted as 'existential anxiety'), it is designated as another given of human existence, applicable to all.

Weixel-Dixon describes this quality:

Angst hovers in the background of all of our activities. It is sometimes dim, occasionally intrusive, but it seems impossible to pinpoint the exact source;

it is everywhere and nowhere. . . . It is Being itself that un-nerves us . . . *it could all be otherwise.*

(Weixel-Dixon, 2017, pp. 21, 22, italics original)

When we make contact with this contingency aspect, when we appreciate that all that we believe, value, presume, and assume is rooted in very tenuous premises, we can become uneasy. We experience the limits of our knowledge and the precariousness of the basis for our choices.

Anxiety, as a feeling, and angst, as a condition, are also related to freedom and choice and will be revisited in discussions of those elements. At this juncture, we can understand that this tripartite correspondence between the three aspects described (uncertainty, angst, and anxiety) can give rise to avoidance strategies or to creativity and an embrace of the challenges that these aspects provide.

It may also be evident that to view anxiety as pathological is a misunderstanding of the nature of the phenomenon. Anxiety is related to angst, as defined earlier. It is the ontic response to an ontological issue and holds the possibility for a creative, and modifiable, engagement with the ineluctable condition of uncertainty and the dis-ease it prompts. To 'remedy' this experience would be to deprive the existent of their opportunities.

Likewise, it is misjudgement to differentiate between 'neurotic' and 'real' or 'normal' anxiety:

Anxiety is an aspect of Being . . . it is the ground on which a spectrum of fears . . . reveals itself.

(Cohn, 2007, p. 81)

Furthermore:

(There is) . . . an ontological meaning to the ontically varying spectrum of fears and phobias.

(ibid., p. 124)

All anxiety, all fears, have a basis in our awareness of the contingency of our existence, and in how groundless are the meanings and assumptions we adopt in order to navigate our way through the storm that is life.

## Some examples of how this theme may be manifested in practice

An avoidance of the experience of uncertainty, and the anxiety it produces, may be demonstrated in an attitude of apathy, or ambiguity. Members may communicate, by word or behaviour, that the groupwork 'doesn't matter', or that there is no clear understanding of the purpose or meaning of the group. Such confusion can often serve to impede commitment and interaction.

Alternatively, in an effort to control the anxiety, members may become very 'busy'. This might be displayed in demands for more prescribed exercises, preferably brought by the therapist (because they are the one who 'knows' what is supposed to happen). Such an imposition lessens creative and spontaneous interactions and dilutes responsibility.

The members may insist on a 'program', a structure that organises the sessions, thereby providing a predictable process. Such rigidity and predictability minimise the risk of 'surprises', which cannot be controlled or predicted and may therefore be threatening.

In keeping with the threat of inherent uncertainty posed by the meeting, members may seek to control or monopolise the conversations or, alternatively, conform to the stated intentions of the more controlling members.

Such acquiescence may serve to relieve members from being instrumental in deciding the direction of the group. They may, for a time, avoid sharing in responsibility for the quality of the group (a shared responsibility, as discussed previously) and thus escape being identified as the source of disappointment or conflict.

Do members seem sedimented, or defensive, about their points of view (demonstrating a need for certainty or 'absolutism')?

Do people frequently voice suspicions of others' intentions (trust issues, uncertainty of knowing another, attempting to minimise the risk of intimacy) or insist that they definitely know how 'others are' (thereby objectifying others, denying their changeability)?

People will feel uncertain about the group experience. They may question: will it be useful, will I fit in, and do I have anything to contribute? Such concerns are common, and appropriate, and the therapist may, at an early meeting, point out that such notions are perfectly suitable for consideration and discussion.

These anxieties and fears are all also relative to the nature of relatedness, as considered previously, as well as those givens of change, choice, freedom, and time. The correlations of the implications for practice are often widely relevant and applicable, as will be demonstrated as we work our way through the universal concerns of humankind.

## References

Cohn, H.W. *Heidegger and the Roots of Existential Therapy*, 2007, Continuum, London.

Spinelli, E. *Practising Existential Psychotherapy*, 2007, Sage Publications, London.

Weixel-Dixon, K. *Interpersonal Conflict, an Existential Psychotherapeutic and Practical Model*, 2017, Routledge, London.

# Chapter 14

# Freedom, choice, and change

There has been substantial discussion of the existential givens of uncertainty and angst, and the particular (ontic) response to these in the form of anxiety and fear, but also of the more salubrious responses of creativity and opportunism.

It would be nearly impossible to separate the givens of freedom and choice, as they are so closely enmeshed; these also bear a significant relationship to angst and anxiety, as we will discover.

It was previously proposed that we are distinguished from objects by virtue of the fact that we 'care' about our existence. Humans *query* their very being because, at some level, we recognise that it could all be otherwise.

This is one of Heidegger's central themes with respect to existence in its entirety: 'why is there something rather than nothing?' (Polt, 1999, p. 1).

This capacity to ask 'why do I live', and *how* shall I live, are ethical considerations, but perhaps more importantly, these reflections indicate that we have a choice in how to respond to the questions. Where there is choice, there is, at least, some measure of freedom.

Freedom, and the concomitant element of choice, is a way we engage with the future. We look to exercise our agency in making choices that will bring about a future aligned with our intentions. We want the current situation to *change*, but, as we have seen, the desired change may not actualise in precisely the manner we hoped for, or it may correspond to what we hoped for but not with the anticipated satisfaction, or the desired change occurs with the anticipated results, which, at a later date, turn out to be a disadvantage or a downright mistake.

Certainly the inverse can be true as well: today's 'mistake' morphs into a beneficial occurrence subsequent to the original decision; these conversions can continue indefinitely. This changeableness is experienced with some trepidation, as it becomes clear that *we cannot actually know ahead of time what is the 'right' choice at any given moment*. In this position, we can feel disempowered.

Additionally, our freedom is not absolute. It is bounded by the effects of previous choices we have made: the options we abandoned, the alternatives we *killed*, come back to haunt us.

This circular process of choice and change, followed by the 'birth' of new options or possibilities, is noted by Cohn:

> Whenever we make a choice, we create a situation with new 'givens'.
>
> (Cohn, 2002, p. 122)

This quote references a different kind of 'given' than those universal conditions reviewed here. This given reflects the boundaries or limitations that are the consequence of our own agency.

In the act of choosing, we 'transcend' our current situation by engaging with 'what might be', but all too often, our choices are based on situations from the past. We seem to believe that the past can help us anticipate the future; while this attitude may be appropriate to a scientific endeavour (but not always), it is less useful in the consideration of human affairs.

Maslow suggests:

> I am convinced that much of what we now call psychology is the study of the tricks we use to avoid the anxiety of absolute novelty by making believe the future will be like the past.
>
> (Maslow, in May, 1969, p. 31)

There is a notion also that the past, or rather our memory of it, has a (nearly) deterministic quality with reference to 'informed' decisions. This is called into question by phenomenology, as we shall see. May puts the case precisely:

> Memory works not on a basis of what is there imprinted; it works rather on the basis of one's decision in the present and future. . . . Let it be underlined that one's present and future – how he commits himself to existence at the moment – also determines his past. That is, it determines what he can recall of his past, what portions of his past he selects . . . to influence him now, and therefore the particular gestalt his past will assume.
>
> (May, 1958, p. 88)

Perhaps this perspective can be recognised as a process that more closely resembles our experience of how we make use of our interpretations of past events.

So we are free to make choices, which will affect our future as well as that of others, without confidence in historical data, without certainty that the desired effects will ensue – in which case we may be faced with making yet *another* choice, *and* we will be held accountable.

So it is that freedom is both a burden and a blessing: even with all the anxiety, would we eschew the privilege? Even if we wanted to, it is impossible; we cannot avoid choosing, as even that strategy is a choice. Hence this dramatic claim from Sartre:

> man is condemned to be free. . . . Condemned, because he did not create himself, yet is nevertheless at liberty, and from the moment he is thrown into this world he is responsible for everything he does.
>
> (Sartre, 1948, p. 34)

The effect of this condition of freedom is that humans shape their world, and themselves, in the choosing. We seek to actualise the possibilities that reflect our values, our aspirations, for ourselves and others. In doing so, we 'exist', as defined earlier: we 'stand out' from nothing.

Perhaps one of the most consequential effects of exercising our agency is that we create ourselves in the process:

> In the long run, what is really chosen is *oneself*. It is out of its decision that the self emerges. A self is not given ready-made at the beginning. What is given is a field of possibility, and as the existent projects himself into this possibility rather than that one, he begins to determine who he will be.
>
> (Macquarrie, 1973, p. 185, italics original)

This assertion is echoed in the work of Sartre, when he claims that 'existence precedes essence' (Sartre, 1948, p. 28). Something very similar is suggested in Heidegger's proposal that 'the essence of Dasein lies in its existence' (Heidegger, 1962, p. 67).

This tenet is also the source of deeply felt isolation. As an agent with contextualised freedom, I am ultimately responsible for the choice and the outcome; I have no excuse, because even if I referenced external, social, legal, or even divine sources for guidance, it was I who interpreted this information.

Additionally, this responsibility is not just about one individual. Our responsibility stretches indefinitely throughout the inter-subjective matrix. What I choose can affect innumerable others, and the values implicated in the choice are righteously available to anyone who shares those values (for good or otherwise).

Here we have arrived at the juncture of choice, freedom, and responsibility: this is the appropriate point to address the notions of authenticity and Bad Faith, as they are issues that reflect the connection among the trio of aspects under review.

'Bad Faith' is a term employed by Sartre (1969), and authenticity a phenomenon described by Heidegger (1962), but the two are not directly equivalent. For the sake of this discussion, we can consider the elements that are similar between the two concepts.

Both Bad Faith and inauthenticity refer to the denial or attempted evasion of the givens of human existence. The former more frequently references that of freedom, the latter focuses on those that illuminate human beings as entities comprised of 'possibilities'. Cohn proposes that this means 'Dasein' (human beings) 'owns a capacity for . . . being open to its own Being' (Cohn, 2002, p. 87); this would indicate the full complement of existential aspects.

When we attempt to ignore or disown the issue of freedom, for example by attributing our decisions to the influence of culture or to the deterministic power of the past (social or personal), we are demonstrating an article of Bad Faith. If we display an attitude that suggests that we can 'keep all options open', without acknowledging that choice, and time, can and do kill off some options, then we are in a 'fallen' state (Heidegger, 1962) and thereby 'guilty' (of inauthenticity).

To stand in an authentic position, we must 'take hold' of the conditions of our existence and purposefully ('resolutely'; Heidegger, 1962) engage with the existential aspects. To exercise Good Faith, we must choose to choose, knowing the limitations of our freedom and accepting the consequences nonetheless.

It is in these events of 'meeting', or engaging with, our existence that we enjoy the greatest latitude of freedom. We are free to choose *how* to engage, and we do so knowing that we may have to re-choose, again and again.

We also recognise that every choice closes some possibilities: it is necessary to acknowledge that we cannot 'have it all'. When we say 'yes' to something, we say 'no' to something else, and the inverse holds true as well. Choice involves *loss* as well as possible gain. The guilt referenced can be exacerbated if, or when, we 'refuse' to risk or attempt to abdicate our agency; this kind of guilt is associated with the fact that we cannot actualise all our possibilities, and we must choose to relegate some of them.

This is the source of 'existential guilt': we always lag behind' our possibilities and execute potentialities with every move, every action.

The premise of 'falling', or failing the call to engage with being, is ineluctable: if there was no possibility of Bad Faith and inauthenticity, there would be little nobility in rising to the challenges that being 'ready for anxiety' (Heidegger, 1962) poses for us. This readiness is not a striving – which in fact is a tactic that works against an authentic positioning – but rather an 'openness', the state of being 'unlocked' (Cohn, 2002, p. 89). Authenticity is an *attitude* that positions us for a particular kind of engagement with the world.

It is important to recall that we exist in a with-world: as we grapple with the various aspects of being human, our involvement is with *all, and everyone*, that meet us at any given moment, pending any choice and decision. Authenticity is not an *internal* quality but a state of being that occurs in the in-the-world, *among and between* the many contacts and engagements we have with our world.

To exist authentically, even episodically, and to adopt a stance in 'good faith', is to be the pro-active author of our life: not necessarily in terms of circumstances, which are not always under our control, but in terms of the attitude we take towards the universal aspects of human existence.

## Some examples of how this theme may be manifested in practice

To what extent do members take responsibility for the groupwork, and for their own lives? How is this demonstrated?

There may be evidence of people taking 'too little' or 'too much' responsibility; this may be in an effort to deny culpability, in the first instance, or to control the process and the outcome, in the second case.

How do group members engage with expressions of regret and guilt? Can they reflect on the part they play in the generation of these feelings, and appreciate that these have a positive aspect as well as being uncomfortable? These feelings are a consequence of the ability to choose and also of the vulnerability inherent in actualising some options and sacrificing others.

When there are expressions of feeling 'trapped' in a decision, is this recognised and worked with (not just placated)?

Do members offer information, or advice, and to what purpose?

How active and/or passive are members in the decision-making process within the group? *How* do they participate? Can people reflect on and articulate the values served in deferring or imposing? This will certainly also have some bearing on how they wish to be seen by others, as well as how they hope to manage relationships.

How and when do members, all or some, defer to the therapist when choices are considered? Do people frequently 'harvest' opinions on their predicaments, looking for the 'right' choice?

Do members seem 'stuck' in making or avoiding decisions? There is sometimes a lot of confusion when making a decision. This can be positive, as there is a lot of possibility in confusion, or it can be a means of delaying making a choice in the hope that circumstances will change, and they will be relieved of making the decision. Nonetheless, procrastination *is* a choice and comes with its own problems.

## References

Cohn, H.W. *Heidegger and the Roots of Existential Therapy*, 2002, Sage Publications, London.

Heidegger, M. *Being and Time*, 1962 (trans. J. Macquarrie and E. Robinson), Blackwell, Oxford, UK.

Macquarrie, J. *Existentialism*, 1973, Oxford University Press, Oxford.

Maslow, A. 'Existential Psychology: What's in It for Us?', in *Existential Psychology*, 1969 (ed. R. May, R.), p. 31, McGraw-Hill, New York.

May, R. *Existence*, 1958, Basic Books, New York.

Polt, R. *Heidegger, an Introduction*, 1999, UCL Press Ltd., London.

Sartre, J.P. *Existentialism and Humanism*, 1948 (trans. P. Mairet), Methuen and Co. Ltd., London.

Sartre, J.P. *Being and Nothingness*, 1969 (trans. Hazel E. Barnes), London, UK.

# Chapter 15

# Death

From the very first second we claim life, or life claims us, we are candidates for death. It has been noted that death is very democratic in this regard.

It seems impossible to even conceive the word without also conjuring its complement: life. Our attitude towards our death, as well as that of others, is inextricably bound to our attitude towards life.

Death represents loss: loss of oneself, loss of others, and loss of any power or control that we might be able to muster in the course of living. It is the ultimate boundary, immovable and indifferent to supplication. The great loss can be represented by any loss: the single senior woman who is inconsolable over the death of her canary is mourning *all* loss, and the ultimate episode that awaits oneself, and all loved ones.

The event of one's own death as a biological and psychological episode remains incomprehensible; it is this ineffable quality that promotes anxiety.

Feifel agrees and takes it even further:

> There is truth in the idea that the unknown can be feared more than the most known, dreaded reality.
>
> (Feifel, in May, 1969, p. 67)

The concern generated by this anticipation is found in every culture. Ritual, religion, society, and art are all endeavours that reflect, both directly and surreptitiously, the anxiety and fascination this phenomenon holds for us.

This does not preclude the possibility of some kind of equanimity, or even acceptance, of this situation. There are people who die heroic or meaningful deaths, some widely known and others that expire in private. Boss comments:

> there are old people who are able to die as peacefully and willingly as children, for they have used up their existence by actualising all of its essential relational possibilities.
>
> (Boss, 1979, p. 121)

We can experience the death of others, but we cannot experience our own death: this deepens its mystery and power over our imaginations. We recognise this final event as something that is truly 'mine' alone, even though we realise it may affect others; others cannot relieve me of this episode. *My* death happens to me uniquely; it is absolutely unable to be shared. What *is* shared, and is communicable, is how we engage with this inevitability.

'Death' in terms of the abandonment or disappearance of options that then render them impossible to realise has previously been noted in the themes of choice and freedom and of uncertainty. Anxiety with respect to these issues is certainly evident in this related concern as well. Death also represents our inherent finitude: even if we lived forever, we cannot 'have it all'. Not all options are available at any given moment in time or in any circumstances that are free from the impact of the will of another being.

Death has been described as a possibility and an eventuality. The juxtaposition of uncertainty, as to 'when', with the inevitability of the event poses a dramatic contrast between what we do not and cannot know, and what we can and do know with all assuredness. It seems we live out our entire lives contending with both affects.

The thought of non-being, at least in the human form, never really escapes our awareness, in spite of the many diversions life offers. Heidegger comments on our status:

> Dasein covers up its ownmost Being-towards-death, fleeing in the face of it.
>
> (Heidegger, 1962, p. 295)

If we 'flee', as Heidegger suggests, where do we go?

We seek respite from the anxiety with a number of defences against the awareness of our mortality. These can be projects advantageous to the world at large, as in works of art or acts of heroism that provide our existence with a lasting significance (though rarely permanently). Unfortunately, acts of a less salubrious nature can also garner us a profile that may serve, to some extent, to challenge the fleeting presence of a single human life.

But, too often, we seek shelter from the awareness of mortality in strategies that serve as a stranglehold on expansive living.

In his Pulitzer Prize-winning *The Denial of Death* (1973), Ernest Becker discusses at length the association between death anxiety and 'life' anxiety. We attempt to 'cheat' death by refusing to fully live. Becker proposes:

> The irony of man's condition is that the deepest need is to be free of death and annihilation; but it is life itself which awakens it, so we must shrink from being fully alive.
>
> (Becker, 1973, p. 661)

(Otto Rank and Paul Tillich entertained very similar views in their works.) We sacrifice some of our potential, some of our possibilities for a fuller life, in order to ward off death: a little bit of dying in manageable doses.

We do this by immersing ourselves in the commonness of everyday life; we distract ourselves by immersing ourselves in the 'they':

> We are driven by anxiety to drown ourselves in the trivial, the social, in all the ingredients of an inauthentic existence.
>
> (Warnock, 1970, p. 57)

This is the human being in flight from engagement with their predicament. It is relevant to all of the givens that are reviewed here and, in each case, is the condition of inauthenticity. To make the point again: 'falling', or the inauthentic engagement with the givens, is *inevitable.* Our agency lies in *how we meet these* unavoidable aspects, as Cohn argues:

> our conflict with what is given and our reluctance to accept our freedom are intrinsic aspects or our existence.
>
> (Cohn, 1997, p. 127)

These avoidance tactics are also the basis for what is often described as 'psycho-pathology', which in its simplest form might be described as

> a graceless, inefficient mode of coping with anxiety.
>
> (Yalom, 1980, p. 110)

But there is some comfort in these mechanisms; we can 'buffer' the raw exposure to the source of anxiety by 'keeping busy'. As suggested earlier, this busy-ness can produce positive results, as in the case of art, but it becomes detrimental when it becomes a rigid strategy that dictates how we live without allowing for change and pro-active choice. Change must be acknowledged if we are to authentically engage with life, and choice must, inevitably, be made on the basis of a novel horizon, if we accept that our freedom is contextualised by our past choices and current situation.

In fleeing, we eschew the 'novel', the spontaneous, because they remind us of the 'unknown' but certain eventuality. We deny or ignore our potential because it brings to light our individuality, the uniqueness that results in that most isolating inevitability.

The thinking is: too much living can bring the conclusion sooner; better to sac-rifice some possibilities than hasten the dreaded episode:

> A small death, after all, is better than the real thing.
>
> (Yalom, 1980, p. 135)

So, what is the alternative option to 'fleeing'? And what benefits might there be to a choosing a different manner of engaging with the anxiety?

It was previously noted that striving for authenticity can be another form of deception: what is proposed instead is that authentic existence is 'not an escape from the world, but a way of existing in it' (Polt, 1999, p. 90).

We are summoned out of the 'they' via a 'call of conscience': this is an event, an episode, in which we acknowledge our responsibility for our actions and *choose to choose*, thus engaging with our freedom (situated as it may be).

Heidegger calls this attitude 'resoluteness':

'Resoluteness' signifies letting oneself be summoned out of the 'they'.
(Heidegger, 1962, p. 345)

We break free from our immersion in the 'they' and reclaim our existence; however, we will inevitably 'fall' again.

An authentic engagement with existence does not guarantee happiness or preclude suffering (and an inauthentic attitude may not provoke suffering, either). The acknowledgement of one's own death, in the sense that it is recognised as a possibility at any given moment, and therefore qualifies me as a 'being-towards-death' (Heidegger, 1962), can produce edifying effects.

Barrett describes this possibility:

Though terrifying, the taking of death into ourselves is also liberating: It frees us from servitude to the petty cares that threaten to engulf our daily life.
(Barrett, 1962, p. 225)

And Becker echoes:

We are liberated towards making our lives our own by our willingness to 'stand naked in the storm of life' (Becker, 1973, p. 86), and to embrace the certainty of a very personal death.

## Some examples of how this theme might be manifested in practice

It can be very useful to conclude sessions by expressing the 'hope' that we will meet again; this emphasises that every session could be the last.

This ploy is reminiscent of Yalom's proposal to 'nurse the shudder' (Yalom, 1980). Therapists do not have to invent means of instilling an awareness of death anxiety and all its ramifications; we need only to reference it, to point it out when it becomes apparent. This will be represented in themes like finitude, limitations, boundaries both natural and contracted, and issues around time and embodiment, as well as narratives about the actual physiological event of one's own or another's demise.

There may also be reflection on the meaning of one's life, or that of others, and the expression of regret for options not chosen, people 'lost' to death or separation, or time wasted. It is important to consider how the group engages with these common dilemmas: do they advise, perhaps thereby avoiding their own anxiety, or do they offer disclosures as to how they too are affected, thereby acknowledging the shared condition?

This issue may also become topical when members, or the therapist, fail to attend a session, either with or without notification; no promise can provide the certainty that anyone will be available for further meetings.

Members may demonstrate exaggerated proclivities for dependence or independence. Yalom (1980) claims that the first tactic is to seek safety by fusing with a protective power; the second is designated as an attempt to become 'special' in a way that defies the condition of mortality and finitude. These two positions could also be seen as strategies to diffuse responsibility for one's choices and life by immersion in the 'they', as described earlier (a policy often described as 'neediness'), and the second position could be an attempt to be a leader, or a power that controls and subsumes others' freedom, to mitigate the effect of the Other's agency. It is often the case that the group members will comment on their experience of their fellow members' attempts to actualise either status at the expense of their own concerns and at the cost of fostering close relational ties that can provide support without manipulation or subjugation. (This may also be represented in self-effacement or self-inflicted, exaggerated, or feigned disabilities.)

A particular member may also frequently seek advice on difficult decisions, without heeding the counsel or without making a choice. Group members can become frustrated with their efforts to help, until it becomes apparent (to some or to the therapist) that the indecisive member really is not looking for solutions but may in fact be 'refusing to choose' – which is, as noted, an impossibility. In such a case, it is most effective to consider with the person what choice(s) they *are* actively making, and why; this refers them back to their own agency. This refusal to proactively actualise one's potential is a refusal of the 'loan of life' and a denial of one's responsibility.

## References

Barrett, W. *Irrational Man*, 1962, Anchor Books, New York.

Becker, E. *The Denial of Death*, 1973, Free Press, Simon and Schuster, New York.

Boss, M. *Existential Foundations of Medicine and Psychology*, 1979 (trans. S. Conway and A. Cleaves), Jason Aronson, Northvale, NJ, and London.

Cohn, H.W. *Existential Thought and Therapeutic Practice*, 1997, Sage Publications, London.

Feifel, H. 'Death: Relevant Variable in Psychology', in *Existential Psychology*, 1969 (ed. R. May), McGraw-Hill, New York.

Heidegger, M. *Being and Time*, 1962 (trans. J. Macquarrie and E.H. Freund), Blackwell, Oxford.

Polt, R. *Heidegger, an Introduction*, 1999, UCL Press Ltd., London.

Warnock, M. *Existentialism*, 1970, Oxford University Press, Oxford.

Yalom, I. *Existential Psychotherapy*, 1980, Basic Books, New York.

———. *Theory and Practice of Group Psychotherapy*, 1995, Basic Books, New York.

# Chapter 16

# Meaning, meaninglessness, nothingness

The meaning of 'meaning' is particularly elusive. It is one of those notions that we understand but ultimately cannot define. Part of the problem may be that it is 'referential' – it refers to the significance of something – but then, it might be recognised that as soon as we turn our attention to anything (or anyone), that focal point becomes meaningful in some fashion. When the meaning of something or someone is described, it is revelatory *of how we understand* that something or someone. However, we shall come to appreciate that these assignments of meaning are impermanent.

It becomes obvious, on reflection, that things can be meaningful without necessarily being 'important'. Polt observes that

> *everything* we encounter is meaningful to us, to some degree. Even a piece of trash that I briefly spot out of the corner of my eye has meaning for me – otherwise, I would not have noticed it at all.
>
> (Polt, 1999, p. 25, italics original)

Meaning may also indicate that something or someone is valued, but not necessarily in a 'good' way. For example, I may value my dog as a reliable and lovable friend, and I may value the neighbour's cat as a vicious, petulant creature: each has a value and a meaning, and these meaningful assignations indicate, indeed disclose, my understanding of and relationship to those entities.

But these understandings, these meanings, are not mine alone.

We experience the world, not as a collection of discrete items, but as a totality, something that 'holds together'. We experience it as meaningful. But we do this as a social group, not as a collection of individuals (Bracken, 2002, p. 90).

So, meanings, as represented here, may provide a sort of organising principle. I know a hammer is meaningful, if I need to build something; but this meaning of a hammer may change if I need to use it as a weapon. But the meaning isn't something I create outside of a *context*; it is a meaning I choose from those available in my understanding, which itself has a social basis.

Bracken explains this condition as he describes the meaning a particular flower holds for him. This appreciation can occur because of his human physiology, which includes sight, but also because he has available the 'idea of a flower and the notion of beauty' (Bracken, 2002, p. 89).

He goes on to suggest:

> I experience the world with words, beliefs, emotions and patterns of thought that come from the social world in which I live.
>
> (ibid.)

To further emphasise this point:

> So we construe meaning, assign value and significance, as we are 'situated', that is, within the world as a 'sphere of meaning'.
>
> (Polt, 1999, p. 72)

In the previous chapter on freedom and choice (Chapter 14), there was some consideration of Sartre's declaration that 'existence precedes essence'. This proposal was relative to how our situated freedom, encumbered as it is by our factical conditions, as well as our capacity for choice, shapes our shared world and is the foundation for the actualisation of the 'self-in-the-making'. More will be discussed about the notion of the 'self', but at this juncture, it is important to note that the declaration cited also indicates 'lack' of materiality, or structure, to the 'self'. This is also designated as the 'nothingness' that constitutes human beings, or 'Dasein'.

It is this absence of solidity, or substance, which is the essence of freedom:

> His freedom is defined in terms of his own potentiality.
>
> (Warnock, 1970, p. 94)

As suggested previously, we are beings-towards-death, acting in ways that seek to actualise a future to which we aspire: we are not determined in the way that objects are. We are not 'driven' or motivated by historical precedents. We stretch forth towards our possibilities: we are always, in this sense, 'ahead of ourselves'.

And in every choice, every action, we reveal our meanings and values. In this regard, Sartre proposes that:

> To choose between this or that is at the same time to affirm the value of what is chosen; for we are unable ever to choose the worst.
>
> (Sartre, 1973, p. 29)

This premise suggests that we always make the 'right' choice, in that whatever we choose is in the service of implementing the meaning and values that serve our purposes, our 'projects'. The 'right' choice may not be the 'good' choice, or the morally correct option, but we *can only* opt for those actions that *seemingly* support our intentions.

And as we are 'condemned to freedom' (ibid.), so are we condemned to meaning:

> Because we are in the world, we are condemned to meaning.
>
> (Merleau-Ponty, 1962, p. xix)

This quest for meaning focuses on the meaning of human existence in general, and it certainly concerns the meaning and value of *my* life in particular.

As reviewed in the chapter of uncertainty (Chapter 13), we are anxious in the face of the vagaries of existence: we prefer to 'know', with some degree of probability at least, that our choices are right, that our values and meanings are well founded and can serve as the basis for navigating our way through life. But the absolute assurances we crave are simply not forthcoming, so we are again challenged with a tenuous foundation for living, finding meaning, and choosing. Even those with religious beliefs are aware (or should be) that faith is a shallow premise if not infused with doubt: the biblical story of Abraham and Isaac has its counterpart in most religious texts and is a prime example of the quality of true faith.

This concept, that we inevitably construct meaning and choose values, indicates that we are, paradoxically, thrown into existence without a given meaning. The condition of life for human beings is foundationally 'meaningless'.

This is a complaint often expressed in therapy: 'life is meaningless, why bother?' But even this denunciation is revelatory: why pose the question if there is no meaning to be found? It is of 'concern' that 'life has no meaning'.

It is understood, then:

> Thus, the therapeutic task is . . . to jointly describe and analyze the meaning the client assigns to his experiences . . . this work of analyzing is not exclusively rational. It includes all that is corporeal, emotional, cultural, relational, even spiritual . . . and beliefs about a personal philosophy of life. If a person comments that *the issue of life philosophies does not interest him*, then that is his life philosophy.
>
> (Martinez Robles, 2015, p. 210, italics original)

Having clarified any such personal philosophy, there can be further description and reflection on *how this perspective is lived, and the consequences thereof.*

Again, we ineluctably construct meaning: we cannot bear the abyss of nothingness, or an existence that is 'rudderless'. Even if we adopt a system of morality, it is a choice, originating in our agency, and we could always be in error: even so, we 'stand without excuse' (Sartre, 1948, p. 34).

But it is necessary to note that however we engage with this aspect of existence, as well as any of the others, we are never relieved of the angst that is part and parcel of being a finite, free, nothingness-bearing existent.

The choice to embrace the construction of meaning allows us to at least attempt to realise a life aligned with our values; we cannot, in good faith, abandon our fate to other forces. If our intentions do not work out, at least we are in a position to take up the challenge, again (and again), as our own responsibility and as the absolute source of the guiding principles that we choose to promote and, some-times, modify. A creative engagement with life allows for review, reflection, and sometimes *revelation and reformation*. This is a project that is never completely finalised, although it comes to an end.

## Some examples of how this theme might be manifest in practice

Many people feel they are at best disadvantaged and at worst suffering from some neurosis if they are not confirmed and confident in their chosen pathways. It isn't necessary or useful to contest this view, but it can be effective for members to dis-cuss their own experiences of choosing, re-choosing, and changing the directions and intentions of their projects.

It is also appropriate to inquire how the person's values and meanings will be realised or impeded in the choices they are considering or already acting upon. Are they invoking meanings, values, and purposes that they would die for, or live for?

Boredom, apathy, and expressions of uselessness and ambiguity are often indicators of a struggle with this issue (as with other aspects as well). It may be the case that individuals restate and repeat the assurances provided by others that their current choice(s) is the 'right' one; or they endlessly review conflicting or ambivalent counsel offered by others about the foundations for the decisions under consideration. This is sometimes a way of 'buying time' (which can never be recovered) or of keeping 'options open', as if this in itself is not already a choice that bears significant meaning and value.

When individuals query, 'what is the point?', it is an appropriate moment to ask how they will know the answer to this question. It may become apparent that the challenge is in fact to act, without assurances beforehand, and only then will there be an opportunity to evaluate the result. The answer to such a concern lies in the future, when the individual has excluded some possibilities and realised others.

If members seem to over-indulge in expressions of guilt and regret, this too can be a means to avoid the new challenge. The next episode in life may also be disappointing, or it may be the occasion in which our values and purposes come to fruition. We are burdened with choosing yet again, but blessed with the freedom to do so.

When individuals discuss or reveal inalterable situations, are they prone to despair and hopelessness, thereby avoiding their responsibility, or can they enter-tain, with the help of others, that the situation presents an occasion on which novel values and meanings may be adopted or integrated? Can they also consider how others, both intimate relationships as well as wider social contacts, might be affected by their predicament?

Do members demonstrate a predilection for conformity to accepted norms (social, familial, or cultural) in an effort to avoid the risk of choosing for themselves? Or display a reticence to accept that others have credible meaning-related views and activities (they may frequently disparage others' values)?

Compulsive activities, including seeking therapy or total commitment and immersion in a cause or a crusade, can provide at least temporary shelter from the anxiety of being the source of meaning and choice (certainly not everyone who is engaged in philanthropic works is acting in Bad Faith).

When a meaningful activity becomes unavailable or comes under close scrutiny and is found to have lost its value, there can be a 'crisis of meaning'. Does the group pacify the individuals expressing this dilemma, thereby avoiding a similar discovery of their own? Or are they able to explore the predicament for the novel values and meanings it presents them with?

## References

Bracken, P. *Trauma, Culture, Meaning and Philosophy*, 2002, Whurr, London.

Martinez Robles, Y.A. *Existential Therapy, Relational Theory and Practice for a Post-Cartesian World*, 2015 (trans. B.C. Duckles), R.R. Yaqui Andres Martinez Robles, Mexico.

Merleau-Ponty, M. *Phenomenology of Perception*, 1962 (trans. C. French), Routledge, London.

Polt, R. *Heidegger, an Introduction*, 1999, UCL Press Ltd., London.

Sartre, J.P. *Being and Nothingness*, 1973 (trans. H. Barnes), Routledge, London.

———. *Existentialism and Humanism*, 1948, Methuen and Co. Ltd., London.

Warnock, M. *Existentialism*, 1970, Oxford University Press, Oxford, UK.

# Chapter 17

# Embodiment and spatiality

As with all other givens of existence, our awareness of our body can be a source of anxiety. 'It' is not always under our control, and we can be surprised, alarmed, and disappointed by 'its' performance or condition.

Ernest Becker famously proclaimed:

> the body is a universal problem to a creature who must die.
>
> (Becker, 1973, p. 164)

Becker goes on to consider what might be the real significance in a child's question about sex:

> He wants to know why he has a body . . . and what it means for a conscious creature to be limited by it.
>
> (ibid.)

Certainly this is a concern that persists throughout life. We know we are going to die and experience our finitude in so many ways, but we don't want to believe it or be affected by this truth. It seems absurd, in keeping with Albert Camus' perspective, that we are entities of both untold potential and finitude.

Here we can understand that embodiment represents the ultimate boundary: when our bodies cease to function, all human possibilities are extinguished, and we are 'finished'. The word 'represents' in the previous sentence is pertinent. We don't actually experience our death; we may endure a process of dying, but the final moment is 'beyond' us. The final moment is never entirely under our control (on occasions of unsuccessful suicides, it is sometimes revealed that the specifics of the attempt were not, in many ways, what was expected).

Our body makes us aware of the impending event: we fall ill, are injured, and may lose mobility or faculty, and we can see signs in the ageing process that portend our fate.

The language that we use with reference to our bodies is telling. As suggested at the beginning of this chapter, the pronoun 'it' designated our corporeality in an objective sense; but, of course, my body is something I 'am' as well as something

I 'have', as has been pointed out by both Gabriel Marcel and Maurice Merleau-Ponty. We experience our embodiment in episodes of pain and pleasure, and we take our body for an object when we try to employ it as a tool or need to analyse it in terms of 'malfunctions'. However, we can never completely objectify ourselves, as it is always 'I' who is experiencing whatever I encounter. There is always a subjective element.

Boss references Jean Paul Sartre's view and remarks on this latter situation:

> People do not simply possess their bodies as they do the tools they make themselves; they actually 'exist' their bodies.
>
> (Boss, 1994, p. 128)

How we 'exist our bodies', how we are able (or not) to reach, to touch, to move, and to use objects (etc.) will have a bearing on how we are able to affect, and engage with, the world.

But it would be a misunderstanding to suggest that we are 'just' bodies, employed as a vehicle for the 'mind': we are psycho-somatic entities.

Body and mind are two aspects of our being, each different in its manifestations. They are never apart but always respond simultaneously, though often with different intensity, to whatever situation they find themselves in (Cohn, 2002, p. 54).

It is possible, therefore, to reflect on and discover the related meanings, values, and assumptions we hold about any experience via an exploration of either or both physical and mental phenomena; it might be said that whichever realm is foreground may become background, and vice versa.

We are being-in-the-world incarnate:

> It is through my body that I can perceive the world: I have a relationship with everything I perceive. Being embodied also allows me to act upon and in the world, and for the world to engage with me in like fashion: it is a 'mode of participation in a world'.
>
> (Macquarrie, 1973, p. 95)

Furthermore:

> My perceptions are always subject to interpretation: they are therefore neither 'wholly physiological nor wholly psychological'.
>
> (Macquarrie, 1973, p. 73)

More will be said of this when phenomenology is reviewed, but it is these value-laden interpretations, based on sensory input, that inform and support the decisions we make and the actions we implement. *How* we participate in the world is a matter of choice, informed but not determined by the interpretations we make and the values that support these interpretations, and with reference to our situated freedom.

It should also be noted that we do not 'exist' our bodies in a purely objective sense. For example, we may claim extensions to our bodily form, as when we say we feel that the horse we ride or the car we drive is an 'extension' of ourselves. Likewise, we may have distorted perceptions of our physical form, as in eating disorders; or amputees may have sensations of a 'phantom limb', a body part that has been removed or altered.

Spinelli summarises these experiences:

> Our image of our bodily self . . . is not a reflection of what is truly there, in a physical sense, but is . . . the reflection of what we *believe* to be there.
>
> (Spinelli, 1989, p. 87)

This belief, common to us all to some extent, may be challenged by others' perception of us. Others may see us as overweight or underweight, contrary to our own assessment, or homely when we think of ourselves as beautiful; these differing views may be dismissed or accounted for in some way or partially or fully adopted. As with various aspects of how and who we are, others' experience of ourselves will have an impact on our existence, in obvious and in obscure ways.

Being-in-the-world is also a spatial experience for an embodied being, but it is difficult to precisely define what is meant by 'space' itself. Macquarrie notes that in the context of an existential analysis, that is, a description of the lived experience, it might be outlined thus:

> Like the world itself, space is neither subjective nor objective. . . . If we begin with the unity of being-in-the-world, then we are beginning with the existent as already spatial.
>
> (Macquarrie, 1973, p. 97)

He goes on to acknowledge that our appreciation of space is grounded in our bodily experience:

> Space is from the beginning organised in terms of our bodily participation in space.
>
> (ibid.)

Up, down, ahead and behind, forward and backward: these are the objective designations that emanate from a lived experience of bodyhood.

We humans, incarnate as we are, *occupy* space, at specific points and destinations. We cannot physically be in more than space, one place, at a time. This seemingly obvious statement has profound implications: our view, the horizon we scan, the periphery available, is very limited by the space we occupy at any given moment. Again, we are confronted with our finitude.

Additionally, we experience our spatiality in context: some things in our field of perception are 'near' or 'far'; this positioning may change according to my movement, and my view will again offer a different perspective.

But there is a proposal that we are not absolutely confined by our spatial incarnation. We can be 'open' to what draws us to a space; we can imagine the space to which we travel. In a vignette in which a vacation cottage is remembered and visualised, Boss comments on this 'openness':

> the very fact that we can visualize something distant shows that we are capable of having something that is not optically perceptible before our eyes, and that we can easily be somewhere besides where we are physically.
>
> (Boss, 1994, p. 91)

He goes on to explain that 'being *there*' is a modification of what we can be open to. We can be receptive to what is not materially present by redirecting our attention away from 'being *here*':

> When we visualize something, we establish a relationship to the thing itself, not to some mere objective representation of it inside us.
>
> (ibid., p. 92)

Once again, we find ourselves on the 'outside', in the world, with all that we encounter and with all that we can visualise and be open to.

It should be noted that this discussion implicates another aspect of existence, that is, temporality; as has been suggested, the givens of existence *are all* always 'there'. Boss concludes his discussion with this very point:

> In speaking of the spatiality of existence as a merging into relationship with what has been, what now is, and what is expected to be, we have already come upon the intrinsic relationship of temporality to spatiality. Past, present, and future are terms indicating something temporal.
>
> (ibid., p. 93)

However, it should be noted that 'now' can be relevant to many people, whereas 'here' cannot. In this manner, we are always a part-*of* (our community) and apart *from* (other beings), as Bugental suggests (1992).

Finally, we cannot complete this discussion on embodiment without addressing the issue of sexuality.

Sexuality as an aspect of embodiment is related to numerous other givens: relatedness, meaning, uncertainty, freedom and choice, and language immediately spring to mind. It makes sense, it would seem, that elements of our sexuality will be referenced in our reflections on any of the existential themes: how we describe our gender and how this aligns or not with others' perceptions or expectations; how we value sexuality and behave, or not, in accordance with these values and meanings. How do we embody forth sexually, with love and tenderness, in mutuality? Or does our sexual way of being indicate a need for power, control, or destructiveness? In what ways do we communicate our sexuality, or ignore or suppress it?

But there remains a debate as to what 'sexuality' is, a question Merleau-Ponty entertains at length in his seminal work, *The Phenomenology of Perception* (1962).

In reviewing this treatise, Smith-Pickard and Swynnerton warn against, and in fact deplore, the kind of restricted designation that is all too common:

> Sexuality thus becomes reified as a defining characteristic of an individual rather than remaining at the level of description of a fundamental aspect of intersubjectivity, as it would be seen from an existential perspective.
> (Smith-Pickard and Swynnerton, 2005, p. 50)

The diversity of opinions on this and related topics is robust and public. It is hoped that the enquiry and the dialogue will continue.

## Some examples of how this theme might be manifest in practice

How do members 'exist' their bodies? Do they claim more space than others, or less? Do some people persistently call attention to, or focus their own attention on, the condition of their body?

It may be noticed that members move their chairs or other furniture in the room to accommodate themselves or others. What might this mean in terms of the relationships among the members, as well as to the therapist, and additionally to the 'space' of the environment?

If it is agreed to keep an 'empty chair' for an absent member or facilitator, how do people engage with this event?

*How* communication takes place is the basis for meta-commentary, which will be described in a later discussion, but there is much to be learned in observing and considering gestures and facial expressions in the course of communications. Non-verbal communication is also demonstrated in modes of dress: is this ever reflected upon in terms of group participants?

Are members able to recognise and work with the biases and assumptions made by virtue of 'appearance'?

Do people touch each other, in greeting, departure, or in expressions of compassion? Is this practice, or the absence of it, noted?

Do members disclose problems or concerns with age, illness and health, sex, death, and other issues related to embodiment?

Suicidal ideation and attempts can be a means of 'conquering' death anxiety; is this an event engaged with sensitively and courageously, or do members pacify the person offering the disclosure or try to minimise the intention of such an attempt or idea?

Most people engage in some sort of self-harm, be it lack of exercise, over-work, or addiction. These issues will implicate other concerns of life: success and failure, need, desire for love and attention. Are these issues acknowledged, and do others share their experiences and views on this topic?

## References

Becker, E. *The Denial of Death*, 1973, Free Press, Simon and Schuster, New York and London.

Bugental, J.F. *The Art of the Psychotherapist*, 1992, W.W. Norton and Co., New York.

Boss, M. *Existential Foundations of Medicine and Psychology*, 1994 (trans. S. Conway and A. Cleaves), Jason Aronson, Northvale, NJ, and London.

Cohn, H.W. *Heidegger and the Roots of Existential Therapy*, 2002, Continuum, New York.

Macquarrie, J. *Existentialism*, 1973, Penguin, London.

Merleau-Ponty, M. *The Phenomenology of Perception*, 1962 (trans Colin Smith), Routledge, London.

Smith-Pickard, P., and Swynnerton, R. 'The Body and Sexuality', in *Existential Perspectives on Human Issues*, 2005 (eds. E. van Deurzen and C. Arnold-Baker), p. 50, Palgrave Macmillan, London, UK.

Spinelli, E. *An Introduction to Phenomenological Psychology*, 1989, Sage Publications, London.

# Chapter 18

# Emotions

Emotions, feelings, thoughts, and sensations are aspects of existence that are always present simultaneously and are constantly changing.

The word 'emotion' is taken from a Latin verb which means 'to move'. This root indicates a basic quality of emotional experience: it is transitory, ephemeral. It is for this reason that it is more appropriate to say that a person is angry (or sad or happy) than to propose that an individual is 'an angry person'. The second statement objectifies an individual, representing them as 'something' in a static condition; this has been described as an article of 'Bad Faith' in Sartrean terms, a deception that functions as a defence against the nature of inter-subjectivity described previously.

'Attunement' is a term employed by Heidegger to refer to the fact that we always find ourselves being-in-the-world in some way: we are always in a 'mood'. He clarifies this as an '*existentiale*', a given of existence (Heidegger, 1962).

These ways of being-there are revelatory: they indicate how we 'find ourselves' and in what 'state-of-mind' we are existing. These moods (also referred to as feelings and emotions) are to be appreciated as important information about our past, present, and future: how we view these aspects of time from our current emotional experience. Polt comments:

> moods are *disclosive*. .... For example, fear does not cut us off from things –
> to the contrary, it reveals something as a threat.
>
> (Polt, 1999, p. 66)

How and what is revealed in the explorations of our emotional experiences will be discussed in greater depth when we consider phenomenology and hermeneutics and their methodologies. Suffice it to note here that from an existential viewpoint, emotions are a means of participating with all we encounter, indeed, with our entire experience of 'being-here'.

On that notion:

> in feeling I am united to that which I feel, and both it and I are included in a whole.
>
> (Macquarrie, 1973, p. 156)

This references that we are always part of a context: it impacts us, and we affect it in turn.

Most people can recognise that they often have a different emotional experience about a past event than they did on the occasion of that event. We evaluate a past situation from our current assumptions and values.

But it is also very important to understand that emotions belong to the situation in which they are experienced; they cannot be 'transferred' from one time period to another. Similar feelings may occur upon recalling an event, but they are feelings that are current and quite possibly different as well.

This proposal is succinctly stated:

> Feelings cannot be revived in their original purity because they are part of a context that cannot be recreated. . . . The anger of today is not the anger of years ago – whatever its relation to the earlier anger may be – it has a new context and is a different anger. *The possibility of change depends on the realisation that this is so.*
>
> (Cohn, 2002, pp. 62, 121, italics mine)

This recalls a premise that was proposed earlier in the discussion about time, i.e., nothing happens in exactly the same way twice.

And because we have a slightly different 'kind' of anger or a novel assembly of emotions about a past, current, or pending event, we have new information connected to these feelings. We have greater scope for making a new evaluation of the situation and for choosing to be and act differently.

This brings us to the most frequently misunderstood notion with reference to emotion and behaviour: stated simply, emotions do not cause behaviour. A simple scenario might illustrate this.

A group member, Janet, frequently complained that she hated working for a business owner that she described as a bully. The owner passed critical and even cruel comments about her manner of dress and her job performance, all the while insisting it was 'for her own good'. The group members made multiple suggestions as to how to deal with such a character, but it didn't seem to satisfy her. After some review of the experience, Janet commented that if she were to encounter this kind of behaviour in a social situation, a party, for example, she would be more likely to offer a rejoinder to his cruel comments. Another member queried: 'Why aren't you doing this at work then?' Janet's answer: 'Because I really need to keep this job'.

This short account demonstrates that although Janet would feel angry about being bullied in any situation, her behavioural response would be directed by what she *valued*. This premise will be revisited when the function and import of the world-view is explored, but it can be noted that emotions are *the voices of values*.

As indicated, emotions 'move'. They change, and there is more than one occurring at any given moment. It is more appropriate to speak of 'emotions' in the plural:

> Just as our sensory perception or our mental concentration, no matter how sharply focused, is always accompanied by a multitude of peripheral sensations and reflections, so no single emotion ever overwhelms us completely.
>
> (Barnes, 1969, p. 75)

An example of this multiplicity of emotion experience might be that I may feel angry with my partner, but I also feel guilty about feeling this way, and also fearful that my anger might drive him away.

This seemingly contradictory melange of emotions is sometimes referred to as 'cognitive dissonance' in some scientific views, but it is contended that they can be better understood as fragments of a whole Gestalt that is the 'person'. To single out one feeling for reflection is an example of splitting off part of a whole: we focus on one element of the experience, make it foreground, and the background fades until such time as we are prepared to bring it into the foreground, thereby relegating other aspects. This is an example of the dynamic and mobile configuration described previously as a 'Gestalt' formation.

But focusing on one aspect is very different to denying that the other elements exist and have meaning.

As to the therapeutic process, emotions are one aspect of a person's experience that can yield pertinent insight into the value and meaning of intentions and behaviour, but they needn't be 'mined' for expression or exploration. It is enough to enquire *how* someone is experiencing their situation and take the cue for further consideration from their answer. Do they respond with 'I think', or 'I feel', or 'I suppose'? These are all indicators of which aspect is prominent at the moment.

Bugental remarks:

> Emotions . . . are similar to blood in surgery: both are inevitable as the work goes forward; both importantly serve a cleansing and function and foster healing; both must be respected and dealt with . . . and *neither is the point of the procedure.*
>
> (Bugental, 1992, p. 113, italics original)

He goes on to advise practitioners engaged with clients:

> Give as much attention to feelings as they do.
>
> (ibid.)

There will be more discussion on this topic when we consider the contributions of phenomenology and hermeneutics.

## Some examples of how this theme might be manifest in practice

It can be helpful to explore and ask for reflection on emotional experience, if and when it is reported; there is no point in 'excavating' for such material, as it may then be a superficial or forced speculation.

When members describe emotional reactions to other's communications and behaviours, it is an opportunity to discover what it is about these interactions that they find uncomfortable, or helpful, or provocative.

If there appears to be an avoidance of emotional expression and content, this can be articulated and posed as an enquiry as to why and how it affects members.

Often the response to an invitation to explore further may be 'I don't know'. This may be true for the moment, or the person may be reluctant to verbalise their experience. In either case, it can be helpful to enquire about the impediment to considering or communicating their experiences and perspectives, e.g., 'What is your hesitation about revealing your feelings or reactions?'

How do members engage with highly emotional communications? It is very important to ask how such episodes affect those present, including the person who has demonstrated strong feelings. This could certainly, and in fact probably should, include the reaction of the facilitator.

The facilitator should feel at liberty to reveal their own emotional responses to the members, their disclosures, and the group situation. This can be followed up with explorations of the disclosures, with respect to the content, as well as the event of such a revelation on the part of the facilitator.

## References

Barnes, H. *An Existentialist Ethics*, 1969, Alfred A. Knopf, New York.

Bugental, J.F.T. *The Art of the Psychotherapist*, 1992, W.W. Norton and Co., New York and London.

Cohn, H.W. *Heidegger and the Roots of Existential Psychotherapy*, 2002, Sage Publications, London.

Heidegger, M. *Being and Time*, 1962 (trans. J. Macquarrie and E. Robinson), Blackwell, Oxford, UK.

Macquarrie, J. *Existentialism*, 1973, Oxford University Press, Oxford.

Polt, R. *Heidegger, an Introduction*, 1999, UCL Press Ltd., London, UK.

# Chapter 19

# Language

As human existence is described as 'being-with-others', it seems to make sense that language is an essential aspect of this condition.

It can be awkward to 'think' about language, because we are thinking in 'language': it is happening as we are thinking, discussing, discovering. We are engaged, involved, and, usually, unself-conscious in our utterances.

Gadamer comments on this:

> The more language is a living operation, the less we are aware of it.
>
> (Gadamer, 1977, p. 65)

Language is not just about delivering information; it is about *gaining* understanding: the kind of understanding particularly significant for human beings, the appreciation of our shared world, our inter-subjective existence. This kind of appreciation is the result of people *expressing* themselves: those intimations that go beyond words.

The inter-subjectivity of language is noted as an 'essential' feature:

> Whoever speaks a language that no one else understands does not speak. To speak means to speak *to* someone . . . speaking does not belong in the sphere of the 'I' but in the sphere of the 'we'. . . . A second essential feature of the being of language is its I-lessness.
>
> (Gadamer, 1977, p. 65)

So, speaking has a purpose: to be understood. Even if the speaker is intending to deceive, it is an effort to direct the understanding, to form it, to mould it to our intentions. This deception is to conceal some things, and what is spoken is meant to reveal others: there is always an inherent ambivalence in language.

'Revealing' and 'concealing' are intrinsic in the dynamic of language. Heidegger proposed that 'truth' is tantamount to 'unhiddenness': language un-hides, i.e., reveals what is being talked about. But in so doing, there are things *not* so illuminated; they remain hidden, as possible material for further discourse and thought.

Language is grounded in being-in-the-world. It is not a tool of relaying so-called inner experiences or thoughts, but rather the shared and developing understanding of existence:

> Language is fundamental and 'worldly'. . . . In our words we reveal the nature of our experience, which is inextricably bound up with our sense of all that surrounds us.
>
> (Harding, 2005)

Macquarrie offers further insight:

> Language successfully communicates when it lights up for two or more people their being-in-the-world and lets each see what the other sees.
>
> (Macquarrie, 1970, p. 147)

It is important to remember that human existence is always situated: our communications will always be with respect to context. We do not create Being: we engage with it in all its aspects and respond to it. How each of us responds to what we meet will not be the same for everyone; we each have a specific 'horizon' (Gadamer, 1997) from which we view our world. This includes our facticity, the space we occupy at any given moment, and the limits imposed by the very process of being human.

In communication it is possible, through understanding, to achieve an overlap of horizons:

> For Gadamer believed that we can and do gain mutual understanding and that this is through the fusion of horizons, where we acknowledge consensus in our particular worldview.
>
> (Langdridge, 2007, p. 43)

Language is made possible by the fact that we bring a pre-understanding to the encounter. We share a context, to which we are 'attuned':

> In other words, the world we share with others has meaning for us, 'speaks' to us, *before words are used.*
>
> (Cohn, 2002, p. 46, italics mine)

To further emphasise this proposal:

> we do not just invent meanings for ourselves out of the blue, we are part of a symbolic context which is multiple, complex and enigmatic.
>
> (Deurzen-Smith, 1997, p. 82)

These principles imply that meaningful communication is an exploration that may end but is never completed. Much more will be said (!) about this in the review of phenomenology and the related tenets of hermeneutics.

## Some examples of how this theme might be manifest in practice

Do members 'edit' themselves when they speak? Are they particularly concerned about how they express themselves?

Do people use language to coerce, distract, or obfuscate?

Do people feel understood? If not, what gets in the way? If so, how has this come to pass?

Do members listen to other speakers and follow through with comments pertinent to what has been verbalised? Or do they too quickly bring the conversation back to their own concerns?

People may insist that their own views are 'factual', or that their perspective is the correct one: are they able to enter into discussions that help to illuminate and expand their understanding, without necessarily agreeing with others' views?

Is silence tolerated, if not welcomed? Can members reflect on this phenomenon?

How do members deal with what some may perceive as deceitful or purposefully misleading comments?

## References

Cohn, H.W. *Heidegger and the Roots of Existential Therapy*, 2002, Continuum, New York.

Deurzen-Smith, E. *Everyday Mysteries*, 1997, Routledge, London.

Gadamer, H.-G. *Philosophical Hermeneutics*, 1977 (trans. and ed. D. Linge), University of California Press, Los Angeles, London.

Harding, M. 'Language', in *Existential Perspectives on Human Issues*, 2005 (eds. E. Van Deurzen and C. Arnold-Baker), p. 94, Palgrave Macmillan, New York, and Houndmills, Basingstoke, UK.

Langdridge, D. *Phenomenological Psychology*, 2007, Pearson Education Ltd., Harlow, UK.

Macquarrie, J. *Existentialism*, 1970, Oxford University Press, Oxford, UK.

# Chapter 20

# The world-view

The world-view is a construct that provides some conceptual organisation to the varied and mutable ways in which each of us engages with the givens of existence.

The givens of existence, as described earlier, are those aspects of being human common to all cultures and all époques. They are the basis for the common ground that we share; we must all contend with these conditions.

These existential givens are the *ontological* aspects of human existence, and how we engage with them is described as an *ontic* manifestation. *How* each of us, *at any point in time*, responds to these inter-related elements is what makes us unique and is, paradoxically perhaps, a fundamental source of diversity. That we can, and do, vary our responses to these aspects also indicates that the world-view, as described here, *is not a fixed position*.

As suggested previously in the discussion about time, it is proposed that nothing can happen in the same way twice. Time changes everything, and everything changes with time; this includes our perspectives, experiences, and the quality of our responses to the universal conditions.

Spinelli employs the term 'worlding' to more adequately reflect this dynamic:

> Worlding refers to the ongoing, ever-shifting, process-like, linguistically elusive living of being.
>
> (Spinelli, 2007, p. 18)

However, as has also been discussed, change can be an anxiety-provoking event. To avoid the discomfort of acknowledging that our assumptions evidence some contradictions, and that we therefore may have to revise our perspectives, we opt instead to 'sediment' those views. This strategy has its drawbacks, as we shall see.

The world-view construct introduced here is comprised of four categories: assumptions, aspirations, and values *about oneself, about others, about the world, and about the cosmos*.

To be clear: within and among these categories, in the 'living' of these abstracts, we grapple with the existential issues that confront us all.

The first category will include intentions to be a 'self' that one values: aspirations to be 'fair' or 'generous' or 'powerful'. But it is not enough that we think of ourselves in these terms; we need and want others to recognise us, confirm us, in these preferred characteristics. It may be clear that our strategies for bringing about these confirmations are always be welcomed; a tyrant may be acknowledged as powerful, but at the cost of being considered generous or kind. It may also be apparent that sometimes others do *not* support our own estimations of our qualities. This can provoke strained relations at best and outright conflict at worst (although conflict can also be an opportunity, as will be discussed).

What can be significant in terms of understanding the quality of our relationships is to appreciate, and *hear*, how others are affected by our strategies for attaining the affirmations that we so desire.

The second category reflects those assumptions, values, and expectations that we harbour with reference to others: how 'they' should be and act, and not just with respect to ourselves, but to others as well. Some of those others may, after all, be significant to us. To the degree that others share and support these goals, we will have friendly, if not loving, relationships; to the degree that these goals are thwarted, we will have competition and divisiveness.

The third category references the world at large. This might include issues – political, religious, or cultural, like climate change or racial equality; it might also concern those personal attitudes that we consider to be righteous or appropriate, like kindness and charity.

The assumptions, aspirations, and expectations associated with this arena of concern are represented in our *group* projects – personal, professional, and social – that are endeavours in bringing about the global conditions that would advance our intentions and causes. These will not be agreeable to everyone. To the extent that others share our aims, we will have peace and cooperation; to the extent that they are thwarted by other groups or parties, there will be contention and conflict.

The fourth category is comprised of those attitudes, beliefs, and assumptions we have about the cosmos. This will include religious beliefs but also the more grandiose perspectives on 'how things are', as in: 'everything happens for a reason', or 'everything is God's will', or 'the universe is indifferent to human strivings'. These creeds will usually reinforce the values represented in the other categories reviewed, but there is always, in the wonderful complexity of being human, the possibility for ambiguity, inconsistency, and contradiction.

This latter comment is true for the inter-related nature of the all four categories: where one might hope (!) for congruence among the ambitions suggested therein, one is much more likely to find antinomy and discrepancies.

The exploration of these unacknowledged ambiguities, as well of those assumptions and values that are complementary, is a central feature of an existential phenomenological therapeutic approach.

It has been proposed that this clarification of disparities among the attitudes that comprise our world-view, and the strategies we employ to deny these inconsistencies, is a principal concern for the project of existential phenomenological psychotherapy (Spinelli, 2007).

By virtue of this kind of exploration, the so-called cognitive dissonances, or ambiguities and contradictions, are often discovered to possess a rationality that may not be apparent to the casual observer.

The nature of this descriptive exploration will be outlined in the following section. It is necessary to note here that producing or inducing change in clients' world-views is *not* the focus of the therapeutic project. Attention will be directed to how the client *is* at this particular juncture; how and if change occurs is at the discretion of the client. The 'sedimentations' mentioned earlier are those positions that we adhere to, in spite of challenges to these attitudes or evidence that they may not be the most efficacious strategies; these are the first ports of call for descriptive clarifications.

For the therapist to direct or suggest changes in the client's way of being or choosing would be to mitigate the agency of the client: a 'leaping in' that may serve to deprive the client of their existential responsibility.

The notion of attempting to attach permanence to our world-view has been introduced as the strategy of 'sedimentation'. As proposed previously, our existence is fraught with uncertainty and the inevitability of change that we cannot always predict and do not always welcome. In an effort to stabilise our position, we attempt to rigidly subscribe to the values, aspirations, and assumptions that constitute our world-view as if they were *absolute truths*. This serves a few different functions: it allows us to mitigate the uncertainty and concomitant anxiety of life, and thereby apply our perspectives in making choices; it grants us some basis by which to qualify our actions and those of others, and how and if these should be modified; and it provides a means of making sense of our being-in-the-world.

We may attempt to deny the mutability of our world-view. As proposed, that denial serves some function: we would be paralysed by indecision if we were constantly aware of the contingent foundations of our existence. However, it is this subscription to such sedimentation that can also impede necessary or desired changes.

Change requires some shift in some aspect of the world-view. This may happen by virtue of recognition of the inadequacy of our perspectives with reference to some event, or it may occur as a consequence of a challenge thrust upon us by an occurrence beyond our control. In any case, the world-view is always a reflection of how we find ourselves *in-the-world*; there is no intra-psychic mechanism driving our interactions.

Additionally, where there is a shift, or even a seemingly minor alteration in the configuration of the world-view, it will affect all four categories; such is the nature of the inter-related perspectives. A short case vignette may help to demonstrate this effect.

A woman, Helen, who was usually an active participant in the group, was noticeably quiet over the course of two meetings. The members respectfully refrained from comment, at first: then Miles, a fellow group member, tentatively enquired as to Helen's well-being and noted her unusual silence.

Helen, with some obvious relief, recounted an event she had recently witnessed: a motorist had collided with a pedestrian, and the man crossing the street was tossed into the air 'like a puppet'. The driver then sped off.

Helen, suddenly fearing for her own safety, hesitated in moving towards the victim; two other onlookers immediately rushed to his rescue, but Helen was 'frozen' and remained in the same position until emergency services arrived. Also, a number of witnesses fled the scene and appeared to be too frightened or just too busy to take time to offer whatever other assistance or comfort they might have provided.

A week later, Helen heard that the pedestrian would be in a coma for an undefined length of time.

Helen was crying freely by the time she had finished her brief account. The other members offered sympathetic remarks, acknowledging how shocking this must have been; indeed, how shocking it was to hear the story.

At first, Helen was somewhat dismissive of their remarks; she said she didn't feel much comforted by their expressions. Another member asked: how could we help you now?

Helen replied that she felt 'shaken to her bones'. She said it wasn't she who had been so brutally treated: why did she feel so 'broken'?

I asked Helen to stay with this feeling of 'broken'. The others waited quietly; no one even shifted in their chairs.

Helen went on to describe her feelings of shame about how she had behaved; she said she felt deeply shocked at her lack of response. She also described how 'inhumane' the driver's behaviour was, leaving the pedestrian in the road like 'a stray dog'. The witnesses who fled the scene acted in the same cowardly fashion as she herself and the driver had done. Finally, Helen commented that it was 'so unfair, so not right' that a person who had caused no offence would be so tragically affected.

The other members shared some stories of how bizarre and/or shocking events had changes their perspectives. This theme continued for many weeks.

Helen worked though the impact this event had on her world-view. She was shocked at her own response at the time of the event and saddened that she was capable of what she termed 'cowardice'; she was appalled at the flagrant disregard for life and responsibility demonstrated by the driver (who was later apprehended); she was dismayed at the apparent lack of concern and reluctance to 'get involved' evidenced in the behaviour of the witnesses; and she was completely taken aback by the sheer misfortune of the victim, subjected to an event that seemed to have no rhyme or reason.

This latter realisation left many in the group feeling vulnerable and, for a time, helpless.

Helen's expression of 'broken' aptly described the situation she was experiencing: every aspect of her world-view – how people, herself, the world, and the cosmos, *should be*, and *were hoped to be* – proved erroneous.

The groupworked with these issues, considered what it meant to be so disillusioned with one's *own expectations*, as much as with oneself and the world and divine powers: what was one to believe? On what basis can anyone assume, hope, or believe?

Such confrontations with life's contingency can be uncomfortable, but they can also provide an opportunity to review, refresh, and re-choose our attitudes and manner of engaging with our world.

The scenario described is a simplified account of how the aspects of the world-view, all reflections of our being-in-the world, are malleable and inter-relational and depict both the universal conditions and the unique ways in which we each engage with these.

## Reference

Spinelli, E. *Practising Existential Psychotherapy*, 2007, Sage Publications, London.

# Chapter 21

# The contributions of existential phenomenology

Stated simply, existential phenomenology is a philosophical and practical approach to the question of how we experience reality.

This approach, grounded as it is in the thought of Edmund Husserl (1859–1938), was developed further in the works of Martin Heidegger (1889–1976) and Maurice Merleau-Ponty (1907–1961).

The word 'phenomenology' is rooted in the Greek language and is usually translated to mean 'that which shows itself'. The question that arises from such an enquiry as stated previously is: do we experience things as they 'really' are, or do we construe 'reality' based on how things *appear to be*?

Succinctly put:

> Phenomenology . . . is the study of human experience and the way in which things are perceived as they appear to consciousness.
>
> (Langdridge, 2007, p. 10)

Any object (including a 'psychic' object, like a dream) or any person that we *perceive* is subject to interpretation. Every object that we 'meet' is considered for its meaning, for example, for its usefulness or for its threat or contribution to our existence.

This interpretation reflects the context of our experience, both past and present, as well as our intentions for the future.

For example, if I am in a police station and an armed officer walks by me, I may feel relatively safe in his presence because of past experience and current assumptions, but if I am on a dark street corner in a neighbourhood I am unfamiliar with, and a person brandishing a gun is nearby, my interpretation or assessment of the safety of the situation will be quite different.

The consequence of this proposal may seem surprising: that is, we can *never* absolutely 'know' an ultimate reality. We are meaning-seeking, meaning-constructing entities and very much *implicated in every act of interpretation*.

There is a saying, credited to many historical and literary sources, that 'we do not see things as they are, we see things as we are'; this is an eloquent declaration of the former principle. This further illuminates the appreciation that *we are part of the context that we perceive and to which we contribute, and that we then interpret.*

If this is so, there is little room for pure 'objectivity or detachment.

It is also apparent that as we are always perceiving and experiencing 'something', we cannot detach ourselves from our context, which is being-in-the-world. There is, therefore, no separation of being and world; we are part and parcel of the entire context, and, one might say, 'embedded'.

Being-in-the-world can therefore be understood as being-in-relatedness to everything and everybody.

Spinelli designates this premise of relatedness (inter-relation) as 'The First Principle' of existential phenomenology' (Spinelli, 2007).

The implications for practice become obvious:

> It can be argued that existential therapy's focus is not even primarily upon the client *per se*, but rather on the particular ways through which relatedness expresses itself.
>
> (Spinelli, 2007, p. 12)

This would include how the client experiences their inter-relatedness with all aspects of life: objects and other people (and other life forms); and, most certainly, how the relation between and the client and the therapist 'unfolds, and enfolds them both during the therapeutic encounter' (ibid.).

To further the discussion about interpretation and 'reality', we can consider the basic premise of phenomenology, that a 'property' of consciousness is that it is always consciousness of *something*: there is always a 'what' (something) and a 'how' (a meaning or a manner) to every experience. These foci are the components of the process known as 'intentionality', in which we 'translate' the raw unknowable material(s) of the world into 'things', objects that hold meaning and significance for us.

Thinking cannot occur without these elements. We are thinking *about something*, even when this something might be an idea or a belief, for example; we take these psychic objects as things to think about. If we have a belief, it is about *something*. The same can be said for experience: I experience something, in some manner, e.g., good, bad, frightening, comforting, etc.

A common consequence of this act of intentionality is that we respond, and act, as if these interpretations give us access to 'reality'. Such an effect is closely related to the notion of 'sedimentation', discussed in previous chapters (Chapter 20, The world-view, and Chapter 21, The contributions of existential phenomenology).

One of the most striking corollaries of these tenets is with reference to the notion of 'self'.

As you are reading this, you are probably not terribly aware of your 'self'. When attention is called to this, then you become aware of your 'self', reading, thinking, evaluating. When we are involved in activity, there is no 'I': this is an occasion of non-reflective experience or 'straightforward' experience. It is only when we reflect on the experience that the phenomenon of 'I' emerges. This is demonstrated in communications about oneself, such as 'I felt great' or 'I was not myself'. Even a statement about how I feel 'now' is actually an assessment of what I felt *when I spoke*, which is already in the immediate past.

But, as suggested previously, when we reflect on experience, even the experience of being 'me', we ineluctably interpret.

The implications are noteworthy:

> This argument leads us to view the 'I' as being an impermanent construct . . .
> a partial expression of an infinity of potential interpreted selves.
>
> (Spinelli, 1989, p. 84)

We experience others via the same phenomenological intentional process. Others are not 'fixed', static, or finalised identities, either; they can be re-interpreted, re-evaluated, with reference to any and every situation or context.

And this is what, in Jean Paul Sartre's famous assertion, makes other people hell: I cannot be certain that if I am deemed 'lovable' today, that tomorrow I will be appreciated in exactly the same way. As proposed in a Chapter 12, another person can deny me the manner in which I wish and hope to be experienced.

Existential phenomenology, as briefly outlined here, grants us an insight into the nature of experience. However, as we interpret, and re-interpret, all that meets us, we sometimes deny or ignore the plasticity of our values and assumptions and opt instead for an illusion of permanent 'knowing' that impedes the creation of new perspectives and extended comprehension.

In an effort to work with the mutability of experience, existential phenomenological psychotherapists adopt a methodology for reflecting on and exploring perception and experience that can allow more complex meanings and understanding to emerge.

This methodology has been adapted from that first outlined by Edmund Husserl (1859–1938), who was interested in a means of getting to the absolute essence of anything that is perceived.

This aim was not realised, but the method, the 'rule of reduction', can give us a deeper, broader, and more intricate appreciation of our experience. The aim of this process, as it is currently practiced, is

> (to) gain a greater critical understanding of the assumptions at play in a person's lived experience.
>
> (Langdridge, 2007, p. 17)

There are three steps to this approach.

The first step is to recognise and acknowledge, as far as possible, what assumptions we hold about any perception or experience (past or anticipated). These are then 'bracketed': we hold these in abeyance while we continue with the reflective exploration as described here. These assumptions, values, and expectations are never entirely dispelled, nor should they be. Neither do we need to devalue them upon recognising more complex meanings.

An example of this would be what you, the reader, expected this book to be about, and possibly by what means you would evaluate its usefulness or impact. Those assumptions and values would most likely have some effect on your experience. On the other hand, if these anticipatory aspects were 'bracketed', even in part, you would have a different experiential quality of the event.

The second step is to describe, without providing explanation or justification, our immediate experience. Explanation can impede insight; it often serves as a 'conclusion', and no further thought or analysis is expected.

Justification and qualification (good, bad, unnecessary, etc.) may also serve to mitigate the manner in which we engage with our situations. Such hierarchical qualifications can also prejudice us in our reflection on events and experiences, distancing us from the more complex and subtle meanings of our experiences. Thus, the third rule is to avoid, as much as possible, the assignment of significance or priority to any aspect of our account or piece of information.

This latter 'rule' is sometimes referred to sometimes as 'horizontalisation'.

There is one final step recommended by some phenomenological practitioners and philosophers: that of 'verification' (Langdridge, 2007). In this, we consider the most recent hypothesis in light of the original context: does it enhance our understanding? Were aspects of the refined perspective noticeable in the pre-reductive appreciation?

This process can be repeated until such time as we feel it is acceptable and possible to accept a tentative perspective on the meaning and value of the experience.

Such a 'descriptive exploration' can challenge the sedimented views we hold as 'final' or as 'absolute' truths. It also promotes an acknowledgement of the biases and prejudices that 'colour' our perspectives and experiences.

Hopefully, such clarification can also lend itself to a tolerance for the necessity of sedimented views, in ourselves as well as others; we could not make a move, so to speak, if we did not have some confidence in our understanding of how things are.

This approach is, understandably, of great import for both client and therapist. The practitioner must also acknowledge their own biases and seek to bracket them in an effort to more adequately appreciate the client's experiences. The client may be inclined to appreciate that absolute 'truth' and 'reality' are inherently unknowable; this applies to self- knowledge as well.

Such an attitude as described here also promotes a more appropriate understanding of the client's world-view (albeit a 'snapshot' of this dynamic phenomenon). It is often the case that client and therapist discover the antinomies, so-called discrepancies, which attend every world-view. Having reviewed one's values and assumptions, they can be considered for their appropriateness and modified or discarded for more satisfying strategies and choices.

As is probably obvious, all of these descriptive explorations and the effects thereof are relevant for therapists and members of the groups they facilitate.

Everyone will be involved; everyone will be affected. The drama of the work unfolds inter-relationally: the enquiries and the revelations include and will affect all those present, and may impact as well those who inhabit our intimate, social, and global situations, often in ways not readily apparent.

The descriptive experiential narratives that occur between and among group members can be explored via the method outlined: at first prompted by the facilitator, and then facilitated by any or all of the members. The value of such discussion is readily apparent and most often is noted by the members themselves.

The most readily available account that presents an opportunity for this methodology to be implemented is the expression of an emotional experience.

When a member reports an emotionally 'charged' event, they are referencing *something* that happened, and *how* they felt about it. Again, there is a 'what' and a 'how' to the experience.

The question that can prompt consideration of the meaning of the occurrence is: 'what is it about that (particular event) that makes you feel so (angry, happy, disturbed, etc.)?'

Too often, we refrain from posing this question because we assume (sometimes correctly) what the answer might be (thereby suggesting our inquiry is vacuous). However, not only might we be somewhat inaccurate, but more importantly, offering the question allows the speaker to discover for themselves, and consider further, the values and meanings reflected in their experience.

This is the stance of studied 'naiveté'. As suggested previously in this text, phenomenological existential practitioners *aspire* to a position of not-knowing, or 'un-knowing', to whatever extent may be possible.

This probe may evoke a response along the lines of: 'well wouldn't you feel the same?' Such a challenge shouldn't be avoided, but rather answered honestly and briefly. It is true for me that I do not know how I would feel in any speculative situation, and this is usually my response to the question. It is also a potent moment to offer the speaker the opportunity to *tell* me/us exactly how it was for them.

This begins a reflection and exploration of the emotional, physical, and cognitive components of a significant experience.

The emotional elements of the story will reveal the *values* being impeded, or realised, or both. The values, aspirations, and assumptions integral to the worldview will be implicated in any emotionally charged experience.

In fact, emotions are the 'royal road' to the world-view. We are emotional about values, about our intentions for ourselves, others, the world at large, and the cosmos. In this sense, emotions are *not* obstructions to understanding, but, as declared in a previous chapter (Chapter 18, Emotions) they are revelatory of the world-view and how we engage with the givens of existence.

The usual comments, observations, and reflections that are integral to dialogue will suffice to encourage and support the kind of phenomenological exploration outlined earlier. 'Staying with' the emotional declarations will facilitate a continuous 'unravelling' of emotional experience and content. As proposed previously, emotions are 'in motion', and the recognition of one is likely to lead to another.

Each time a different feeling is identified, the fundamental query is maintained: what is it about that (experience) that brings up (fear, joy, sadness)?

There will likely come a time when the person reporting will move away from the emotional review and begin to consider the overall meaning of their experience. Because they have been facilitated in an extensive consideration of the emotional aspects, and the values and aspirations reflected therein, they will have a deeper comprehension of how their world-view informs their choices and in what ways this may be effective and/or problematic.

The aspirations, values, and expectations represented in the four categories of the world-view are the basis of our behavioural choices: we want to preserve, or produce, the results we desire and treasure.

Phenomenology practised in this manner can facilitate a deeper appreciation of how we engage with the world. In a group setting, we may come to understand that although many of our perspectives about our context are shared with our social milieu, we each also harbour distinct biases that serve to inform our choices, values, and behaviours: we are the same, *and* different.

## References

Langdridge, D. *Phenomenological Psychology: Theory, Research and Method*, 2007, Pearson, Prentice Hall, Harlow, England.

Spinelli, E. *An Introduction to Phenomenological Psychology*, 1989, Sage Publications, London.

———. *Practising Existential Psychotherapy*, 2007, Sage Publications, London.

# Chapter 22

# The contributions of hermeneutics

It has previously been proposed that interpretation is ineluctable: we often fail to acknowledge that this inevitability effects a circumscribed appreciation of 'the things in themselves'.

But there are different kinds of interpretations, and these are related to equally distinct notions of explanation and understanding, as we will consider.

Hermeneutics originally referred to interpretations of religious texts. As a corollary to existential phenomenology (both are concerned with interpretive processes), hermeneutics more broadly addresses any aspect of language, written or spoken. It has also been extended to include the 'reading' of people and their experiences (Ricoeur, 1913–2005; Dilthey, 1833–1911).

As has been noted previously, language allows us to describe our experience, which is always *about something*, and *how* that something is experienced. Interpretation is a process of understanding something: something that we wish, indeed, perhaps need, to understand.

It was also argued that the phenomenological method might provide some insight into the assumptions and prejudices that attend every perception and inform every experience. It might have been inferred that such biases are deemed inappropriate, but, in fact, these too are revelatory: they are manifestations of the context in which we find ourselves.

In seeking to interpret something, we start with that with which we are familiar, in order to attempt to understand that which is novel or foreign. As the phenomenon is part of the context in which we currently stand, there is a possibility of bringing contextual understandings, i.e., biases, to bear on the process of comprehension. Such pre-understanding is an effect of previous interpretations and experience and 'will be limited and enhanced by these factors' (Weixel-Dixon, 2017, p. 52).

In this manner, the new is enfolded with the old:

> The knower's own present situation is already constitutively involved in any process of understanding.
>
> (Linge, 2008)

In therapy, the phenomenon that presents itself for the kind of interpretation outlined here is the client's lived experience, i.e., conscious experience. We focus our interpretations, and the ensuing understandings, on that which is concrete – not hypothetical. This does not mean that the understanding is superficial, or ever complete: it can unfold indefinitely. Every new hypothesis, or current understanding, begs another question and calls for further consideration.

For every piece of revealed understanding, a new horizon comes into view: our information is different, our options are variable, and our new perspective illuminates novel and undisclosed possibilities. It is this evolvement of understanding, occurring between and among people, that facilitates the fusion of horizons and promotes cooperation and appreciation.

This 'hermeneutic circle' of answer and question promotes understanding that always stands as a tentative position: this is in contrast to interpretations that seek to arrive at a single, conclusive explanation.

Such an attitude towards reflection and exploration casts a different light on the notion of knowledge:

> Thanks largely to Heidegger . . . Many thinkers now view knowledge not as a static set of correct propositions, but as a continuing search for better interpretations.
>
> (Polt, 1999, p. 41)

With such a description of knowledge, it is clear that there is a distinct departure from the perspective put forward by scientific paradigms:

> For the existentialist the paradigm of knowing is not the objective knowledge of empirical facts sought by the sciences, but knowing persons. . . . When we talk of 'knowing', we imply that understanding has reached a level of adequacy that entitles us to be reasonably certain about its findings.
>
> (Macquarrie, 1973, pp. 133, 134)

It is to be noted that to suggest we know something can refer to a 'degree' or quality of knowing, e.g., vague, deep, superficially, but essentially, our knowledge is incomplete and changeable. These variables in knowing apply to ourselves, to others, to the world, and the cosmos.

As proposed in the chapter 19 on language, we speak in order to be understood. The kind of speaking that best supports the understanding between and among people is 'dialogue':

> 'Being-with' develops during dialogue. The role of dialogue is to communicate meaning through the process of question and answer.
>
> (Moja-Strasser, 2005)

Again, we are reminded of the 'we-ness' characteristic offered earlier by Gadamer.

To clarify further the quality of dialogue:

> The dialogical character of interpretation is subverted when the interpreter concentrates on the other person as such rather than on the subject matter – when he looks *at* the other person . . . rather than *with* him at what the other attempts to communicate.
>
> (Linge, 1977)

To look *with* an Other, we can, to some extent, share the view of their horizon: it becomes, in part, *our* horizon.

In this position, we can share an understanding that might not otherwise have been available; we also can recognise the other-ness of the Other, as well as the aspects that belong to us specifically. The 'other-ness' will also always lead to *misunderstanding*: this may be an episode in the gradual unfolding of meaning and significance.

This is *participation*: it can yield understanding and knowledge that is a product of engagement, not detachment (which is a premise of the natural sciences).

'Truthful dialogue' is a principle discussed in Gadamer's seminal work, *Truth and Method* (2008). He suggests that a dialogue that is *not* directed by the conversants, and that is *not* forced into a particular direction, is more likely to effect a truthful quality that is absent in a more structured exchange. Such free-floating communication is a truly creative venture, in which the participants are active but not leading. The contributions may be uneven, varied, but the speakers 'find' their own way though until the exchange is stopped, although not necessarily 'finished'.

This is contingency in action: the outcome is uncertain and unknowable in advance.

Such a 'meeting' will affect all those involved. One cannot participate or be engaged without being affected.

This manner of discourse is called the 'dialogical attitude' (Spinelli, 2007). This notion indicates that this is not something 'to do', but rather a way of *being-with*.

It is an aspiration, a possibility, which underpins the existential phenomenological approach to psychotherapy and counselling in individual, couple, family, and group contexts.

However, there is a caveat to this process and its effects: what makes this kind of communication effective, and affective, is also what can cast it as threatening: new understanding almost *necessitates* change, and again, such modifications are not wholly predictable.

And there is a further risk:

> Additionally, there is a possible liability in being understood: one's vulnerabilities can be exposed and exploited.
>
> (Weixel-Dixon, 2017, p. 54)

The possible hazards described here give some insight into *why people don't listen*: they may hear something that challenges their way of being. Additionally, people do not engage in 'truthful dialogue' because they may reveal their vulnerabilities and may then be manipulated or judged when these become apparent.

Here we can appreciate what makes relationships difficult. As proposed in a previous chapter (Chapter 12, Relatedness) the other 'sees' me and holds the secret of who I am.

Unlike phenomenology, hermeneutics does not offer a methodology, but, similarly to phenomenology, it proposes an attitude towards understanding and interpretation and promotes a platform for a dialogical relationship.

Interpretations in the hermeneutic sense, whether they originate with oneself (in context) or are offered by another, can facilitate understanding among and between all those involved in the exchange. Such understanding, in turn, provides a kind of knowledge that references relatedness and experience: worthy aims for the therapeutic endeavour.

## References

Gadamer, H.G. *Truth and Method*, 2008, Sheed and Ward, London.

Linge, D. 'Preface', in *Philosophical Hermeneutics*, Gadamer, H.G., 1977 (trans. and ed. D. Linge), p. xiv, University of California Press, Los Angeles, London.

Macquarrie, J. 1973, Penguin Books, London.

Moja-Strasser, L. 'Dialogue and Communication', in *Existential Perspectives on Human Issues*, 2005 (eds. E. van Deurzen and C. Arnold-Baker), Palgrave, New York, and Houndmills, Basingstoke.

Polt, R. *Heidegger, an Introduction*, 1999, UCL, London, UK.

Spinelli, E. *Practising Existential Psychotherapy*, 2007, Sage Publications, UK.

Weixel-Dixon, K. *Interpersonal Conflict*, 2017, Routledge, Abingdon, UK.

# Chapter 23

# The nature of problems and the process of change

As might be expected, problems and dilemmas are seen as consequences of how we are in-the-world: what it means to be human and engaged with the givens of existence.

'Engaged' is a significant choice of word. We are always engaged, in some manner, as the existential givens cannot be dispelled or successfully avoided; we are confronted with the challenges they present on a daily basis, and we *choose* *how* to engage with them.

As existence is described as being-in-the-world, difficulties will be 'located' in the relationship between the person and their context. Their context, and their interpretation of it, will be reflected in their world-view in terms of values, expectations, and assumptions, as outlined previously.

In an earlier chapter (Chapter 10, The existential givens of existence), we reviewed the notions of ontological and ontic: the former designates those aspects of existence common to all human beings, e.g., death, freedom, etc.; the latter is the particular way each of us responds to these givens. These categories reflect, respectively, the general and the specific.

Every account of any event, or any problem, will reference the givens, and as these are all inter-related, there will be more than one implicated.

Cohn outlines how difficulties are relevant to these universal aspects:

> The existential therapist proposes that it is unaccepted aspects of existence itself which are at the core of the disturbance . . . these unaccepted aspects of existence . . . can be warded off in many ways – by denial, evasion, and distraction.
>
> (Cohn, 1997, p. 24)

He goes on to state:

> From an existential perspective there is at the core of many (perhaps all) psychological disturbances a conflict between the 'givens' of existence and our response to them.
>
> (Cohn, 1997, p. 125)

Examples of this might be a person who complains about their tendency to procrastinate; this gives some indication that there is an issue with 'temporality'. The exploration could start with some consideration of their 'engagement' with time, for example, what their assumptions ('all the time needed'), expectations ('I have a lot of time left'), and values ('time is the least of my worries') are. There may also be some unacknowledged attitudes around change, choice, and uncertainty ('how do I know this is the 'right' choice? Why take the risk? I won't make any choice now'). Additionally, there may be some refutation of one's finitude ('if I choose to do this, I have to relinquish another option').

It is probably relatively easy to ascertain the denial and deceptions involved in these statements: many of them indicate an attitude of omnipotence, certainty where there is contingency, and an attempt to abdicate responsibility and the ineluctable burden of choice.

But in any case, it is also important to consider in what specific ways denial, evasion, or distraction *serves* a purpose, and *what that purpose is*. It is likely to be an attempt to maintain something, like a rationale for subscribing to the status quo; or to achieve something, as in the desire to be seen and experienced in a particular way.

In this way, it is possible to discover the meaning and value in *what is being chosen* before moving on to consider what is not being chosen.

Reflection on and descriptive exploration of the world-view is the focus of existential phenomenological therapy. It is by virtue of such an exploration that the values and aspirations we hope to realise in our choices (and behaviours) become apparent. The world-view is a 'snapshot' of our current *responses* to the universal aspects of human existence; the examples given are those in service of denial and evasion.

And there is more: the unacknowledged or denied antinomies, contradictions, and disparities that we harbour in our world-views, as well as the sedimentations that we seek to impose on this ever-changing collection of perspectives in order to deny the uncertainty that comes with inevitable change, may all be revealed to both therapist and client in the course of dialogue.

These sedimentations come at a cost. We abdicate the creative response to life's conditions, a response that breathes vivacity and colour into our lives; we 'play it safe'. This is somewhat understandable: to stand in an *authentic* relation to life's call is arduous, thrilling, seemingly dangerous, and rarely easy.

The notion of authenticity is too often touted as an 'aim' of the therapeutic endeavour, but in the existential phenomenological model, this is not the case. Authenticity is not a goal. In fact, Heidegger indicates that 'striving' for authenticity is an inauthentic strategy (Heidegger, 1962). It is a striving in the effort of 'achieving' a goal, rather than a quality of engagement with life's exigencies.

In an inauthentic position, we are in a 'fallen' state. We are under the spell of 'everydayness':

> It can be difficult and disturbing to face our own temporality and to experience the mystery of Being. . . . Heidegger consistently points to the difference

between this everyday sort of oblivion and a state in which we genuinely face up to our condition . . . he calls this the difference between *inauthenticity* and *authenticity*.

(Polt, 1999, pp. 5–6, italics original)

This 'oblivion' is related to the anxiety and uncertainty of life. We immerse ourselves in the 'they', the common mentality, in an effort to ignore or evade those elements that are uncomfortable or uncontrollable. In this state, we interpret ourselves, and others, in a general sense, in the 'common' sense, and in a 'thing-like' way. As we have noted, 'things' have 'essence' and are not free to do or be otherwise, nor do 'things' harbour awareness of their facticity and finitude.

Such preoccupation is unavoidable: perhaps we are not always capable of wrestling with the call of Being. Heidegger comments:

Authentic Beings-one's-Self does not rest upon a condition . . . that has been detached from the 'they'; *rather it is an existentiell modification of the 'they' – of the 'they' as an essential existentiell.*

(Heidegger, 1962, p. 168, italics original)

This 'modification' is a consequence of the 'call of conscience'. This means that we experience an 'angst', a 'dis-ease', that when paid attention to is a reminder that we are in a state of avoidance.

But the modification referred to does not happen 'inside' a person. It occurs in the relational field:

An authentic deed is not the private invention of an individual, but is the individual's appropriation of a publicly accessible opportunity.

(Polt, 1999, p. 161)

The anxiety aroused re-calls us to reassert ownership of our potentiality-for-being, which includes our mortality, our factical history, and our agency. Ironically, the sources of the anxiety that inclines us to involve ourselves with the 'they' are also the sources for emerging from the 'herd' and for adopting an attitude of 'resoluteness'.

Van Deurzen clarifies this position of Dasein (human being):

It is only when this process of authentication or rather of ownership begins to happen that we may begin to think of Dasein as becoming authentically and resolutely capable of being ready for its potentiality of being . . . not to be thought of as a self but a constant moving forward into the future with an awareness of a past and a present as well.

(van Deurzen and Arnold-Baker, 2005, p. 164)

Inauthenticity doesn't necessarily bring suffering, any more than authenticity promises an easy life. What an authentic engagement can deliver is a deeper involvement in one's own existence: we can open ourselves to all the potential in being human, although some of those possibilities, and eventualities, can be disconcerting and certainly challenging.

Considering the source of disturbances as described here, it is perhaps clear that our greatest latitude in the exercise of freedom is to choose *how* we respond to the universals of human life. Choosing on the basis of our own understanding (limited as it may be, and contextualised as it is) makes us the authors of our own existence. Additionally, as our understanding develops, we can re-choose our current way of being or make a new choice based on a novel perspective: but we are 'condemned' to choose, one way or another.

On this theme, Sartre's proposal is apposite:

> To choose between this or that is at the same time to affirm the value of what is chosen; for we are ever unable ever to choose the worst.
>
> (Sartre, 1973, p. 29)

This assertion indicates that whatever we choose, it is in the service of some intention, some aspiration. Even when we opt for something seemingly 'harmful', or that goes against a claimed value, there is a purpose that is given prominence over other ambitions.

Spinelli offers a succinct statement of the emphases and aims of existential phenomenological therapy that references the kind of difficulties described so far:

> to offer the means for individuals to examine, confront, clarify, and assess their understanding of life, . . . the problems encountered . . . and the limits imposed upon the possibilities inherent in being-in-the-world.
>
> (Spinelli, 1989, p. 127)

The inherent limits are those universal conditions noted in this text: we are finite, as is our understanding; we are in relation to everyone and everything; we are mortal (time-bound and historical); we are free, although this is contextualised; we are anxious in the face of life's contingencies.

All of this has immense implications for group therapy. As has been argued, existence is fundamentally relational; one might appreciate, then, that life's difficulties can be more effectively addressed in the presence, and with the participation, of a number of others.

Medard Boss (1903–1990), a psychoanalyst who developed an existential-phenomenological paradigm based primarily on the works of Martin Heidegger and dealt with 'patients' diagnosed with a variety of neuroses, comments on the inter-subjective nature of so-called pathology:

> Our discussion of human pathology brings us face to face again with the fact that human illness and its treatment are both peculiarly rooted in fundamental

human nature, in man's being-in-the-world and his inherent being-together with others in a shared world . . . in other words, social behaviour is necessarily involved in illness. Consequently, any program of therapy . . . is essentially an instance of social medicine.

(Boss, 1994, p. 283)

# References

Boss, M. *Existential Foundations of Medicine and Psychology*, 1994 (trans. S. Conway and A. Cleaves), Jason Aronson Inc., Northvale, NJ, USA, London, UK.

Cohn, H.W. *Existential Thought and Therapeutic Practice*, 1997, Sage Publications, UK.

Heidegger, M. *Being and Time*, 1962 (trans. J. Macquarrie and E. Robinson), Blackwell, Oxford, UK.

Polt, R. *Heidegger, an Introduction*, 1999, UCL Press Ltd., London, UK.

Sartre, J.P. *Existentialism and Humanism*, 1973 (trans. P. Mairet), Methuen and Co. Ltd., London.

Spinelli, E. *The Interpreted World, an Introduction to Phenomenological Psychology*, 1989, Sage Publications, London.

van Deurzen, E., and Arnold-Baker, C. (eds.). 'The Self', in *Existential Perspectives on Human Issues*, 2005, p. 164, Palgrave Macmillan, Houndmills, Basingstoke, UK.

Chapter 24

# Relational issues

Relational issues are conditions of inter-subjectivity common to the process of group psychotherapy and, indeed, to all contexts of human relations. This term is preferred over the more familiar notion of 'group dynamics', which is often associated with a psychodynamic model and refers to 'intra-psychic' phenomena (even in a group setting).

These conditions can occur at any point in the group process, as they are qualities that can be engendered, lost, re-defined, and re-found. In other words, these are possibilities of relating that are in flux, concomitant, sometimes subtle, and sometimes obvious.

One of the concerns about groupwork most often cited is that of '**safety**'. To understand the significance of this issue, we need also to consider its opposite, that is, 'risk'.

The risk inherent in human relations has been adumbrated previously: the Other can experience me as they wish. I may experience their interpretation of me as critical, unaccepting, and generally challenging. If I feel critiqued for who and how I am, I may refuse to participate or retaliate in like manner by adopting a judgemental attitude of the Other.

If someone views me in a manner that feels depersonalising, for example, by imposing a cultural stereotype to describe or explain my behaviour, I might feel objectified and despair of being treated respectfully and appreciatively. There are very few of us who haven't been subjected to such biases.

However, I may also challenge the Other's view of me. To the extent that open and sincere communication can take place, these prejudices may be mitigated. Such a shift in perspective may start with the acceptance that another may not share my views, but that we respect a difference of opinion, unless the threat is too great to mediate.

When such a challenge is met and worked through, it is likely to evoke a greater degree of felt safety. This is a more solid grounding, as it has been openly addressed rather than simply assumed. Additionally, both or all parties have participated in making themselves safe.

But, as noted in a previous chapter (Chapter 22, The contributions of hermeneutics), prejudices are inevitable, as they are part, and revelatory, of the social fabric in which we are immersed. What can be hoped for is that we recognise the mutability and limitations of our biases.

In groupwork, a few very basic boundaries can be set to contribute to the most fundamental need for physical safety. These will be discussed in later section (Part III), but the emotional risks inherent in relationships are the source of a wide range of anxieties.

'**Trust and cynicism**' are issues that attend every human contact. There are occasions when we 'feel' we can trust someone quite readily; there are other situations in which we are dubious as to whether, or to what extent, trust can be attained.

Then there are those who feel that trust is most often a precursor to disappointment and seek therefore to 'shield' themselves with superficial contacts and relations, but at some cost. By 'shrinking' one's engagement to a modicum of output and input, we drain our existence of colour and variety. The experience of disappointment can be bilateral: our cynicism can also be founded on the likelihood that we can disappoint others, a situation that is an anathema to some.

Disappointment is an occurrence that can test the bonds of inter-personal engagement and commitment. It can be viewed, however, as an opportunity to consider the source of this experience and what values and expectations we hold that supply the basis of this hurtful experience: in other words, how we ourselves contribute to the situation.

Trust can be lost and rebuilt. Communication about the nature of the disappointment, and an attempt to understand the other's point of view, are essential to regaining this confidence. However, it is also imperative to recognise that each of us is also capable of disappointing or betraying the trust of another, even without intent to do so. This is a common occurrence in relationships in which the partners harbour firm assumptions about who and how the other person 'is'. This is a consequence of being viewed, and viewing others, as entities that are *definable*, rather than describable; the latter term indicates something that is ephemeral.

Additionally, 'knowing' an Other implies all the limitations of knowledge and truth that have been previously discussed. We have assumptions about, and expectations of, others that are based on imperfect understanding. As argued previously, we wish for others to be fixed entities, so that uncertainty, and the attending anxiety, is assuaged.

When we inadvertently betray the trust of another, it is necessary to acknowledge that this is *so*, that this is how it is for the other at this juncture: explanations or excuses are not likely to engender a renewal of trust. If we attempt those kinds of strategies, it can discredit the other's experience: this leads to further hurt and feelings of betrayal. An acknowledgment of the pained party's experience is the first step to reviving some level of trust.

Trust can be a basis for intimacy. Both engender some level of appreciation for the Other, and both are forms of shared, if imperfect, understanding.

'**Intimacy**' is like a hothouse flower: it needs nurturing and attention. It will wither if it is not especially cared for. Intimacy must be expressed in word and deed to thrive, but, like many conditions, it is never 'fixed', never static. It seems to be most satisfactory when the experience is voluntary, mutual, and reciprocal.

Intimacy is not born solely of dependency or independence: it requires both distance and proximity. Each of us needs to be 'seen' as a unique being, as well as appreciated for our contributions to our populated existence. We wish to be part of something greater than ourselves but do not want to be subsumed by any network or context (except in cases of inauthentic relations). We long to be 'safe' in our intimate relationships, so we minimise the distinctions between and among us, but then discover that such familiarity does indeed breed disinterest, and we look to someone or something more 'exotic'. This reflects an ebb and flow between the known and the enigmatic.

If we can appreciate that the Other is never totally knowable, we can experience a degree of safety in our close relationships, as well as the excitement that attends the unfamiliar.

A look, a gesture, a spoken word, an affectionate nickname, and of course, sexual bonding are all possible expressions of this inter-subjective appreciation. It extends to friends, family, lovers, and even to those who cross our paths only briefly; it is intermittent and all the more treasured for it.

'**Resonance**' is a concept preferred to that of empathy. The latter is most often employed to designate an intra-psychic phenomenon, rather than an inter-relational quality; after all, there need to be at least two people for such a condition to occur.

Resonance is a meeting, not a mimicking. It is risky, in the ways described previously, and it is enlightening in that it is an occasion of *shared understanding*. As with any understanding, it is finite, but in the horizons that overlap, it is profound, usually comforting, and a basis for cooperation and camaraderie.

This understanding is neither simply emotional nor cognitive: it is a 'tuning in' possible between and among people because we share common ground. We all have some understanding of being-in-the-world; we are all contending with the same issues in life. And it is also the instance where we appreciate that we are also all unique, in terms of the particularities of one's past: we are the same, *and* different.

Resonance is not agreement. It allows for recognition of what is different for the Other and how it is different, as much as what is similar between and among us.

In the context of therapy, Spinelli refers to this phenomenon as 'being-for' the client:

> Being-for the client expresses the existential therapist's willingness to attempt an increasingly adequate 'resonance' with the client's world-view . . . is concerned with the therapist's attempt to embrace the world-view as currently valid and appropriate for the client.
>
> (Spinelli, 2007, p. 109)

Here it is suggested that the accepting attitude of the therapist *validates what is so* for the Other, without qualifying it from the therapist's perspective.

However, the caveat: as argued earlier, being understood, to any extent, can be our undoing. Our intentions and inclinations can be exploited, used against us; it is sometimes the price we pay for seeking community.

'**Collusion**' is a condition that stands in sharp contrast to intimacy and trust: it is a conspiracy of appearances.

Collusion occurs when we seek to deceive in conjunction with others. The intentions of such secret contracts are usually to achieve an outcome that is ambiguous in both effect and liability.

An example of this might be that group members fail to address an issue or a difficulty that is apparent to all but feels 'risky' to open up for discussion: this is the 'elephant in the room' syndrome. The risk might be that it is a particularly painful subject for a member, or members, and no one wants to bear the blame for exposing the sensitive topic; or it is believed that revealing the issue will produce a 'rift' in the comfortable status quo, and the speaker will be held responsible.

A less duplicitous occasion of collusion may be demonstrated in complicity. For example, in a group setting, a therapist might have some indication that two members are involved in a clandestine sexual relationship. The therapist withholds this information in the hopes that the members will themselves discover or disclose this breach of boundaries, or that those involved will confess their arrangement.

Such strategies in withholding information can be hazardous. As with so many other communications and interventions, it is a matter of judgement; if it becomes problematic, there is still a possibility, indeed, an opportunity, to explore both the rationale of the withholding act as well as the consequences of doing so.

'**Competition and collaboration**' are both necessary ingredients for healthy relating. These conditions reflect the fact that any group will fulfil some desires of the members and likewise frustrate some individual ambitions. There is also likely to be some disharmony between the demands and expectations of the various and multiple groups to which any of us belong.

Competition is a contention, in action or word, about what to value: each side, or party, believes they hold the 'worthy' intention. Healthy competition can motivate participants to put forward their best efforts or arguments: if unsuccessful, the strategies or ambitions can be reviewed and/or re-evaluated. Indeed, if competitors make a good case for their position, it is entirely possible that the result will be a compromise, which produces a novel aim or understanding or a reformed 'team'. 'Unhealthy' results are those in which the successor punishes or demeans the defeated competitor.

Collaboration is necessary to accomplish many, if not all, goals in life. Even the most modest intention, like preparing a meal, requires tools and ingredients likely to be manufactured and made available by others, or by networks of other people (if one were preparing a repast in the wild, one would be collaborating with what nature provides!).

Collaboration is an opportunity to be part of something communal, and to participate in the actualisation of shared values. This is the foundation of social order and civilisation. It can even occur between rivals in an effort to achieve a singular common goal, and certainly is likely among and between those that share a more comprehensive affinity.

'**Affinity and enmity**' are not mutually exclusive. As we have considered, it is possible to hold one or the other position at any given time, or some mixture of the two, and we may revise our evaluations at any given moment.

Affinity, including that emotion and attitude designated as 'love', has its advantages and its pitfalls. We more readily make assumptions about those we love and seem to need to 'cement' those perspectives in a bid for stability and certainty. However, love can also be a very 'forgiving' attitude: we make room for the peccadilloes of those whom we so favour.

Enmity can be a productive context in which one is challenged, even contested, and forces us to justify, to ourselves as well as others, our demands and expectations. When disputes are met with a willingness to listen and learn, if not to revise, it can be an enlightening engagement.

Enmity can be destructive when it relegates completely the perspective of the Other: such a position is often detrimental to all parties. An intractable view can severely limit the options for a productive outcome (such an outcome is sometimes described as the occasion where all parties are equally unhappy!).

'**Responsibility**' was reviewed in an earlier chapter (Chapter 14, Freedom, choice, and change); it should be apparent that it is a favoured topic of the existential proponents, as are the related topics of freedom and choice.

In group therapy, it can become apparent that responsibility is an issue *for*, *to*, and *about* everyone in attendance and beyond. In the view of Jean Paul Sartre, we are infinitely responsible for the condition of human existence as a whole (Sartre, 1973).

As group members listen to each other's disclosures about difficulties and struggles, they may discover how to be responsible in their engagement: sympathy and endless suggestions for problem-solving are often met with polite exasperation, if not outright scorn.

'Solicitude' is a Heideggerian term that alludes to a manner in which we contribute to the understanding of, if not the solution to, difficulties in living:

> A solicitude which does not so much leap in for the Other as *leap ahead* of him in his existentiell potentiality for Being, not in order to take away his 'care' but rather to give it back to him authentically.
>
> (Heidegger, 1962, p. 159)

If we can visualise this as an action, it might look as if someone springs in front of another person to encourage them in their search for meaning and to discover the significance of their values and choices.

If we think of 'leaping in' for another person, we can imagine *taking over* their mission to choose and engage authentically with their own existence. This latter manoeuvre is too often in service of our own need to help and solve problems, instead of seeking a tentative understanding of the person's existential dilemma. If we succumb to a need to be 'useful', at the expense of the Other, we may deprive them of the opportunity to be the *author of their existence*, which is the essence of 'responsibility'. We should bear in mind that the consequences of their decisions, in any case, will be laid at their feet, but we may be also be, or feel, implicated.

When group members express a sincere gratitude for the help the others have offered, or dismay at attempts to be of assistance, it can be useful to explore why such gestures are appreciated or how they are inappropriate.

It has also been noted previously that 'no one can do nothing in a group': all those in attendance are responsible, in some part, for the condition of the group. The level of responsibility may not be equal among members, or consistent; as with many qualities, it is dynamic.

'**Power**', too, is a dynamic potential: it flows, it ebbs, it extends, and it can be withdrawn. It can be overt; it can be discrete. It can also be one of those experiences that is only noticed in hindsight, when one has been the focus of another person's strategy.

Power is referenced in two principal contexts: the power to act, to attempt to manage one's own destiny; and as the means by which we can wield influence over others.

When people complain of a lack of power, they are usually focused on one arena in which their aspirations have been impeded; more will be made of this when we look at the nature of conflict. However, most often there are other options for actualising one's values: we too often become entrenched in what is being denied, at the cost of losing what might be achieved.

As in the example given previously, with reference to responsibility, it is possible to *disempower* another if we 'take over' for them. We may, with all good intentions, deprive them of or mitigate their agency and self-determination (although this is always situated within a populated co-existence).

This is the arena in which therapists must exercise caution and critical judgement in their intentions and actions with respect to clients or group members. It can be tempting to impose a view on people that serves to validate our own theories. It is best to recall that theories are based on (falsifiable) assumptions, expectations, and explanations; such an imposition can unduly affect the client's report of their experiences and perspectives, as well as corrupt how these are 'heard'. In such a case, we might describe such an imposition as a misuse of power on the part of the therapist (or any other 'listener').

Due to the attitude assumed in existential-phenomenological practice, it seems less likely that such an occurrence would take place. The phenomenological method assists in alerting us to our biases, and we appreciate that all understanding is contextualised and incomplete. The 'truth' is always a work in progress.

However, it is also possible that one can be perceived as 'powerful', regardless of one's intentions otherwise: accusations of 'bullying' or forceful imposition often cause understandable offense. On these occasions, it can be useful to recall, as argued previously, that it is important to recognise the validity of another person's point of view, without necessarily acquiescing to the characterisation: we are not 'totalised' in that description. Again, there is an opportunity to discover what behaviour, by all parties, has contributed to the perception.

Additionally, it must be appreciated that people can and do attempt to exercise influence over others for their own advantage. Such manipulation may be overt or discrete; it may be inducement to convince or outright forceful attempts, as in coercion (difficult behaviours will be considered in more detail subsequently).

Overt attempts to coerce are readily recognisable. Appeals to values or vanities, threats of withdrawal, and bribes are a few of the usual strategies.

But there are some very mendacious means to manipulate and manage. Possibly one of the most distressing is that in which one person seemingly yields to another's choice, but denigrates the other for exercising their power; this is commonly referred to as 'playing the victim'. The person who acquiesces often attempts to shame the others in the exercise of their choice or will.

An example of such a situation might be when a group member comments that they have 'no choice' in a matter, when, for instance, the group decides to end the session a few minutes early. The communication makes it apparent that the dissenting member doesn't actually want to make a stand for their own position, but opts instead to express their displeasure by reluctantly conceding to the wishes of others. This may lead to the decision being reversed, and those that so capitulate are left with unresolved tensions; more likely, it leads to resentment on the part of those who voted in favour of the move. The 'victim' has plausible deniability for causing any ill feelings, as they declined to openly oppose the option, so the blame for the discomfort is too often shouldered by, or assigned to, those that supported the original choice.

Such strategies should be challenged directly: an invitation to those involved to explore their reactions to the exchange can defuse and clarify the effects of such manipulation.

The misuse of power is a possibility in any human contact: everyone has some power, except in the most extreme circumstances. Sometimes the power is sourced in the potential for debasing or devaluing another person or persons. Few of us are so thick skinned as to be impervious to all kinds of characterisation.

Most significantly, power imbalances cannot be 'fixed' by a well-meaning party. A therapist who recognises a power imbalance that becomes problematic in the group can only bring it to the attention of *all* of the members. and promote reflection and exploration of the qualities of relating that are demonstrated.

We can all become more aware of how we deploy our potential to influence. It is an understandable consequence of the anxiety inherent in the unpredictability of life and relationships, but it must be subject to honest and critical evaluation.

When a few, if not a number, of the supportive and helpful conditions described here are evidenced, the group is likely demonstrate a quality of '**cohesiveness**'.

Yalom compares this property to that of rapport in individual therapy (Yalom, 1995): it is a feeling of being accepted, valued, and supported, a sense of 'belonging' to the group.

This essential ingredient seems to produce a number of effects: appreciation of and adherence to boundaries, an alignment with the expectations expressed in and by the group, a favourable amount of risk-taking in terms of self-disclosure, and a sense of 'we-ness' that is a quality of community.

As good as all this sounds, this principle does not, fortunately, prevent discomfort and conflict. In fact, it *allows* such experiences to be more openly acknowledged, named, and worked with. Members are more likely to feel safe enough to express their dissatisfactions (even with the facilitator) and may come to understand that such difficulties, when explored, can lead to greater understanding and deeper transparency between and among the members.

It is also common that when this quality is present, the members take a greater interest in and responsibility for the functioning of the group.

It is noteworthy that this condition can be a unifying force and provide the bedrock for therapeutic work and authentic relationships.

This review of relational issues is not exhaustive: there are nuances and variations to these conditions and, as suggested, they co-exist and vary in degree and effect.

But it is paramount to recognise that these are qualities that occur among and between us. We are all, as with existential issues, inextricably bound.

## References

Heidegger, M. *Being and Time*, 1962 (trans. J. Macquarrie), Blackwell, Oxford, UK.

Sartre, J.P. *Existentialism and Humanism*, 1973 (trans. P. Mairet), Methuen and Co. Ltd., London.

Spinelli, E. *Practising Existential Psychotherapy*, 2007, Sage Publications, London, UK.

Yalom, I. *Theory and Practice of Group Psychotherapy*, 1995, Basic Books, New York.

# Chapter 25

# Conclusion and summary, Part II

Part II is meant to provide grounding in some of the basic principles of existential phenomenological theory, particularly as it related to group therapy.

The givens of existence, pertinent to all époques and cultures, were reviewed and common examples of how these themes become apparent in the work. By virtue of many of these descriptions, it is also evident that all difficulties, indeed, all successes, reflect the interconnected nature of the existential aspects.

Universal conditions also provide a 'pre-understanding' of our with-world: we are all subject to the same concerns, although how we engage with these will be unique to each of us in some way. These elements can grant us an appreciation of how we are all alike, and how we are also all different.

It is hoped that the material presented here makes it clear that the 'doing' of therapy is essentially grounded in a philosophy of Being. Philosophy grants an understanding of the human predicament, and psychotherapy is a means by which we can reflect and explore our concerns and dilemmas. Addressing this point, May comments:

> The important thing is to *be* existential.
>
> (May, 1958, p. 90)

This caveat reminds us that our practice is not an intellectual exercise but a *meeting* of persons who participate in, inform, and impact upon our shared world.

To 'be existential' is not limited to professional therapists. For everyone and anyone that considers the meaning of life, and of *their* life, and the anxiety that is in fact inevitable and ubiquitous, they stand in relation to the entire menu of existential aspects.

This latter proposal. and those tenets that suggest that our lives are characterised as inter-relational, supports the view that the existential paradigm, as described here, is a particularly appropriate basis for group psychotherapy.

It has also been argued that human existence is not an 'internal' phenomenon. We are rooted in being-in-the-world; all of our thoughts and intentions reference others, our cultures, and our cosmos. Barrett puts it eloquently:

> Man does not look out upon an external world through windows, from the isolation of his ego: he is already out-of-doors. He is in the world because, existing, he is involved in it totally.
>
> (Barrett, 1962, p. 217)

Existential phenomenology, of which hermeneutics is an associated perspective, asserts that knowledge and truth are consequences of interpretation. Hence, these aspects are contingent, as we ineluctably interpret all that our milieu presents to us. Such an assumption can inspire humility and compassion: no one owns the absolute truth, and it would seem wise to heed the validity of another person's, or another group's, perspective.

There has also been some consideration as to what the source of problems is, and, correspondingly, what the nature of 'change' is. It has been suggested that problems reflect a disturbance in communications (which in turn references inter-subjectivity), as well as a denial or evasion of the givens of existence. Change rooted in an understanding of what is to be gained and what is to be lost is more likely to be a 'responsible' choice. We recognise that some values will be com-promised, and which values will be actualised. Choosing is losing: we 'kill' some possibilities in order to give life to others. Again, we are reminded of our fini-tude, and the fact that we must choose in the face of limited foreknowledge and embrace our responsibility and freedom even so.

It may be noted that diagnostics, as applied in medical and psychodynamic models, do not align readily with the views presented here: such categorisations can be dehumanising. Martinez Robles makes this observation on diagnostics:

> As a result, the person becomes a phobic, an anorexic, an addict, etcetera, instead of someone who's experiencing problems or difficulties with a par-ticular situation in her life.
>
> (Martinez Robles, 2015, p. 61)

Diagnostics are divisive: 'sick, 'abnormal', 'irrational' separate some of us from others, with less likelihood that we can understand and help each other. The prem-ises proposed here, that problems are related to the universal aspects that touch us all, promote the possibility that we already share some understanding of each other's difficulties.

Finally, though this text is divided into sections titled 'Being and boing', then 'Doing and being', this dichotomy is not so clearly defined (as is the case with most 'divisions'): they are aspects of a whole, which we might describe as being-in-the-world. The point of this distinction is simply to invite the reader to carefully consider whether, and how, their understanding of what it means to be human informs their way of being-with, both in therapeutic practice and in life.

## References

Barrett, W. *Irrational Man*, 1962, Anchor Books, New York, NY.

Martinez Robles, Y.A. *Existential Therapy*, 2015 (trans. B.C. Duckles), Yaqui Andres Martinez Robles (pub.), Mexico City, Mexico.

May, R. 'Contributions of Existential Psychotherapy', in *Existence*, 1958 (eds. R. May, E. Angel, H.F. Ellenberger), Basic Books, New York.

# Part III

# Doing and being

# Chapter 26

# Forming, maintaining, and ending the group

## Selection of members

The most common question with respect to this topic is: how does one know who to include in the new group?

It would seem apparent that a random group more closely reflects real life – but then again, it may be worth considering whether a group context is the most appropriate for what the client hopes to achieve. It is hoped that there may be some correlation between what the group may provide and what the members need and want but, these aspects are unlikely to be entirely aligned, and indeed, there will be alterations in these conditions.

So, perhaps a better question is: who may not be willing or able to make use of the group context, and why? The focus of this question concerns the well-being of both the individual seeking help and the group itself.

The answer to this question supplies the most efficacious and ethical grounds for both inclusion and exemption.

Most practitioners favour some kind of interview and orientation for those wishing to participate in group therapy. This strategy serves to inform and prepare applicants in terms of their expectations, and to address any misapprehensions they may harbour about the process.

It is advisable to set the date for the group to begin before interviews are advertised and conducted. This will preclude some applicants who cannot attend on that date and also give an indication of how long the members will have to wait for the group to start. It is also prudent to explain what will be discussed in the intake interview and that the suitability of the client for the group, as well as the aptness of the group for the client, will be the principal consideration. It should be made clear that the meeting and the results will be kept confidential.

An intake interview is also the best means by which to pre-empt 'drop-outs'. There is evidence to suggest that when candidates are well-informed about the process of groupwork, the absentee and drop-out numbers are minimised (Yalom, 1995). However, this begs the question as to what is meant by 'well informed'.

The most obvious query for the candidate is what they hope for by participating in the group project. It is rare that the expectations are inappropriate: most people are hoping for a relief of their suffering, including those effects of their own predicaments that are visited upon others they care for. An aspiration to be 'cured' or 'unconditionally' accepted could be warning signs that the applicant may not be suited to the group context; these are expressions that indicate a predilection for 'getting' rather than a more balanced view of giving and receiving.

The benefits and risks possible in the group setting will be further outlined subsequently in this chapter, but the intake interview should address those issues specifically queried by the candidate.

One of the most common concerns mentioned by candidates is that the facilitator or other members will apply pressure for disclosures about personal issues, which the member may not be prepared to offer: a 'forced confession' scenario. It can be pointed out that everyone develops trust in their own time and to differing extents: trust is not a static condition, and neither is safety. It is understandable that people will be reticent when they feel vulnerable.

There is also often some uncertainty as to how one's difficulties with anxiety, or compulsive behaviour, could be addressed in a group setting. In previous chapters of this book, it has been asserted that all difficulties have a social implication: there is often shame or guilt attached to feelings and behaviour that leads to difficulties in trust and intimacy. This inter-related factor can be easily described and noted as a significant aspect of the work.

Frequently there is a concern voiced about the fact that group participants do not have the undivided attention of the therapist, as in individual therapy; there is some discomfort about this aspect, as they will have to 'share' this source of help and healing. Such a concern can be addressed by noting that sharing with group members difficulties and issues similar to one's own can offer hope, comfort, and a deeper understanding.

Candidates often wonder, with some trepidation, whether they will 'fit in', considering that the group is composed of strangers, and whether and how they can benefit from such interaction. It may be apposite to clarify that, in these circumstances, there is an opportunity to understand at a deeper level how we affect others, and to offer to others one's own experience of their behaviour in return. These responses and interactions with those who are initially 'strangers' can then be compared to the relationships, with intimates as well as those less well known to us, encountered in our general milieus.

There is also usually some fear of 'losing control' over one's emotions, or of being destabilised by the dramatic expressions of others. As proposed earlier, emotions are valuable in discovering what is important in one's life: everyone experiences emotions, and hopefully, the group experience will help in discovering how to express these responsibly and effectively. This perspective can readily be explained to the prospective member.

Such issues should be addressed directly, with very basic responses to the concerns expressed, but with the caveat that groupwork is sometimes difficult and challenging. This is so for everybody in attendance, and it is precisely these kinds of sometimes awkward or even painful processes that can prove to be enlightening.

It is also important to note that when a sense of appreciation and belonging is produced among members, it can be a potent source of hope and encouragement.

It is not possible, or desirable, to totally assuage these anxieties: they are appropriate and understandable.

It is also helpful to bear in mind that they, and we, are not there to learn how to manage bullies, do-gooders, or any other such characterisations (these are deeply depersonalising profiles). We are there to participate with others, with as much candour and courage as can be mustered at that juncture; and when we cannot face a challenge, it is an opportunity to consider what this is about.

Such a message indicates that all qualities of interaction are accepted, indeed encouraged, except those that are blatantly abusive.

If an interview is conducted, there are a few options for eliciting the kind of information that would be useful in considering if the person can use this group effectively at this time in their life.

To begin with, the client may be asked to write a brief response to a few pertinent questions, in essay form, ahead of the actual interview meeting.

I refer to Foulkes for the basis and rationale of these:

> I then find it useful to ask him to write on *his own ideas* about his condition, *his own theory* as it were of his disturbance, and furthermore *his expectations*, in particular *how does he think these conditions can change* and how is this change to be brought about?
>
> (Foulkes, 1986, p. 28, italics original)

The intention, as proposed by Foulkes, is to ascertain the applicant's attitudes about the nature of their problems, and about the source and probability of possible change. It also, at an early juncture, provides the applicant with the opportunity to be *involved* in their assessment and in clarifying what it is that they want and need to change.

These lines of enquiry can be further expanded upon in a face-to-face meeting, if there is time and opportunity to do so.

The implications of these questions may be apparent: the answers are likely to disclose to what extent the person can acknowledge responsibility for their situation, and for implementing the expressed desire for change.

One might imagine how varied these replies would be. Some people will assign the blame for their difficulties to circumstances or other people; some answers will reflect that the longed for modifications should be supplied by other people changing *their* behaviour in order to accommodate the aggrieved or suffering party.

The candidate may also demonstrate the extent of their sympathy for other's discomforts as contrasted with their own needs for compassion and understanding; this is an indication that the person understands the positive effect of reciprocity and relationship.

With any and every introduction or interview with a client, I am always tuned in to whether the client is 'other-oriented': do they ask me how *I* am? Do they enquire about the nature of the difficulties of others and consider whether they themselves have something to contribute? Are they aggressive in their enquiries, or are they too compliant and conciliatory? Can they withstand a gentle probe of or challenge to their own views?

Do they depart from the interview with the hope that this project can be an opportunity to give as well as receive, and to understand as well as heal? I have some confidence that how a client is with me can be a good indication of their suitability for group: on those occasions where I have doubts or serious concerns, I consider my own biases and vulnerabilities before I come to a conclusion.

I believe that the questionnaire and the introductory meeting are a good representation for the candidate of the kind of inter-personal stance that serves as a foundation for the groupwork.

The profile of a desirable candidate might be succinctly described as 'a person who can both contribute to and benefit from group' (Friedman, 1994, p. 37). This rule of thumb, though seemingly general, alludes to an attitude of inclusion rather than exclusion with reference to possible members.

Yalom asserts that the most common scenario is one in which a limited amount of 'de-selection' takes place. The facilitator excludes only those candidates that would seemingly reap little benefit from the situation: a rather subjective evaluation, but then again, he proposes that the process of selection is anything but elegant or precise (Yalom, 1995).

If the interviewer believes that the applicant is not suited for groupwork, the applicant should be so advised. It may be apropos to suggest that *this* group is not suitable, or that this group at *this time* is not in accordance with their needs or expectations.

However, as relatedness is an aspect of every human existence, it would seem that everyone could benefit from, and make contributions to, a therapeutic group of some description at some point in their life.

Subsequent to his experiences in military hospitals, Foulkes offered this opinion:

> it would look that under peacetime civilian life conditions one could equally well treat patients as a group together without any particular selection.
>
> (Foulkes, 1986, p. 39)

This strategy would certainly most effectively replicate the situations most of us find ourselves in: members of multiple groups that have no particular selection process other than common aims and interests, and values that attract us in one way or another.

## Practicalities and boundaries

It is advisable to discuss with those applicants that are likely candidates for the group the proposed practicalities and boundaries. Those boundaries that are intractable should be made clear: if necessary or appropriate, specifics of conduct can be clarified, as in no threats of violence or physical coercion. There may also be rules specified by the facilitator, or by the contracted venue, as in prohibition of smoking or drug use.

The first issue should be confidentiality. On this aspect, it seems sufficient to outline the basic parameters. It is likely that the person attending the interview will have questions about the extent, or exemptions, of this standard. As it is a topic that will inevitably come up in the group itself, I describe a very basic expectation and recommend that the candidate bring any further considerations to the first group meeting.

It is also highly likely that other group members will have something to say about this issue, even if they have all been briefed as to the proposal. It may seem obvious to some, but to many it appears to be an unwieldy expectation. There are individuals who will query with whom, and in what circumstances, they are allowed to discuss the communications and events that take place in the group. This will be the first of a few, or many, 'boundaries' or 'norms' that the group will work through, and not just once. This is to be expected as a welcome and inevitable part of the group process.

I had a ten-week group that spent a great proportion of their time thrashing out this particular element of our agreement. I commented, at intervals, that it seemed this contractual condition was related to trust issues among the members. The group worked well with this difficulty; even though all members were never completely aligned in their views, they agreed to differ despite the fact that this put a few people 'on edge', as they were never absolutely sure about the agreement particulars. There was some accord around the notion of 'respectful' handling of members' interactions and anonymous attributions of these. This was an example of how the intentions and needs of the individual are sometimes thwarted by those of the group, much the same as in most social contexts.

The initial interview should also present the applicant with a rationale for the proscription against sub-grouping (or any kind of socialising external to the meetings). These kinds of discrete alliances among a few members, or even two, may or may not have romantic basis: it seems to be an inevitable phenomenon in any case.

The hazard presented by the formation of such a coalition is that the values and intentions of the coterie may take precedence over those of the group. In fact, the frustration of not having one's aspirations served by virtue of concession to, or competition with, the group expectations is the most common foundation for the sub-group, who will ostensibly support each other in the face of obstructions to their own pursuits.

In conjunction with the phenomenon of sub-grouping, even as it remains covert, there is often a 'sense' among group members that some people 'belong', while they themselves, or others, do not. This can be a disruptive phenomenon, especially for more reticent members, and can lead to 'drop-outs' if some people feel excluded.

However, there is a case to be made for the therapeutic value of the sub-group: if they disclose their alliance, and are willing to discuss what difficulties within the group led to the coalition, others might be relieved of their guilt (believing they were the cause of the rupture) and/or become aware that others share a vulnerability around disclosing their own dissatisfaction about the groupwork, about other group members, or about the facilitator.

Yalom remarks on this phenomenon:

> the therapist may actively point out functioning, but shifting, subgroups of members who share some basic intra- or interpersonal concern and urge that the subgroup work together . . . and share the risk of disclosure as well as the relief of universality.
>
> (Yalom, 1995, p. 329)

If the therapist alludes to the sub-group event before others do, it must be an observation delivered with equanimity and without threat. It should be offered for consideration and discussion among all members; as is suggested earlier, there may be more than one sub-group in operation, and being critical or punitive will not encourage others to come forward.

To be succinct: the explanation for the prohibition of sub-grouping is most effective when presented in terms of the negative impact on other members; additionally, it may also be made clear that if the breach of policy does occur, it should be disclosed for the benefit of all.

The logistics of group formation can be covered in the intake interview, for example, the number of members in the group, the duration and frequency, the venue, the expected commitment in terms of attendance, and the number of weeks or months this contract will last.

Additionally, the facilitator/organiser of the group will determine, according to their preference, whether the group is a 'closed' group, which maintains (hopefully) the original membership, but in any case does not replace anyone who leaves; or an open group, which allows for members to be replaced, thereby retaining the original number of participants.

Either situation can be assigned a time frame with reference to contract, or the 'open' group may be organised without a specific date for termination (this is more often employed in organisational settings, like hospitals or prisons).

For a closed group, eight to ten members in addition to the therapist is a common arrangement, although the venue is also a determining factor. This somewhat arbitrary number will also be relevant to how much administrative duties a facilitator is encumbered with.

There is much debate over the pros and cons of both formats. In my estimation, it appears than a closed group more readily fosters deeper disclosure and trust; however, the open format more closely resembles our western experience of mobility, diversity, and blended families. Additionally, in an open group, there is quite a bit more administrative work for the facilitator, e.g., interviewing new applicants, exit interviews, and advertising or broadcasting the available placement. The choice will be informed by the practical options and contexts, as well as by the experience of the facilitator.

If there is to be an assessment of some description upon the dissolution of the group, it should be outlined in the intake interview, and the time frame set for whatever kind of report is to be made. The explanation for reflection and feedback on the members' experience should be offered with reference to the benefit it can provide for the participants, as well as for the facilitator/organiser. This written review should be requested after a reasonable period of time has elapsed, allowing for a thoughtful response from those involved (including the therapist, who may also wish to give some descriptive report of their own experience and views).

As to whether or not these reviews are held in confidence: it would seem that when they are, the offerings are more freely communicated, in terms of critical as well as congratulatory reports. However, it may also be useful for the members to read each other's reports, if that is agreeable to all. There is also the lack of opportunity for response if the summaries are shared, unless this occurs among members themselves. Again, the parameters of confidentiality have to be agreed before this exercise commences.

Once these conditions are explained and agreed to by each member, a brief written contract can be signed by the applicant at the intake interview, and by the therapist. This serves primarily as a reminder, but it does not preclude or guarantee that there will not be further clarifications and negotiations on any or all of these elements. Regardless of how clear the points may seem at the time of signing, almost inevitably there will be occasions where exceptions or misunderstandings arise and need to be discussed in group.

## What and how much to explain

In both the intake interview and the group sessions, it is more effective for the facilitator to invite questions rather than deliver a long and possibly unnecessary speech.

However, a few basic issues are ubiquitous and can be addressed briefly. These will usually be discussed within the group, and variations on these themes will always be topical.

There is often a query about how people can get the most from the group experience. The short answer is it is relative to how much, and in what manner, they contribute. Not every member will be comfortable with disclosing their struggles, and silence, or reticence, is something of a communication in itself.

I also articulate that genuine disclosure can be helpful, to the individual as well as to the group, in that it allows for a sense that we have many of the same meaningful issues: we may handle them differently, and have a variety of emotional reactions to our particular situation, but in a very basic way, we are 'all in the same boat'. This is more commonly referred to as the condition of 'universality'. And, I am likely to offer my own disclosure, at some point, usually in reference to something that occurs in the meeting and affects me.

On one such occasion, there was a member of the group I knew from another context and was someone for whom I held some affection. I also had some suspicion, later confirmed, that this member was suffering from a health condition that might be terminal. In the meeting, the themes around temporality, at first a rather intellectual exercise, led a member to reveal her distress at the recent death of her sister. I realised in that moment that I felt very sisterly towards the woman I knew, and tears rolled down my face, quietly, but certainly noticeable. After a respectful silence, the person to my left asked if I would like to share anything: I replied that I would like to think about it, until the next meeting, and thanked everyone for their concern.

In the next session, I shared that I was facing an imminent loss of a close colleague, and felt moved by the report we heard in the previous session, but I hadn't thought it apt to reveal this so soon after the bereaved member had revealed her own loss. But the fact that I availed myself of the prerogative *not* to share at that moment prompted an energetic exchange about how to be respectful and thoughtful in making disclosures, so they might be received with appropriate consideration.

This was a juncture in which I felt, and I think this was shared, a sense of universality, and the ability of most people to offer sincere sympathy and understanding, which demonstrates the benefits of mutual support. These occasions have an effect on everyone present, even those who may not be as verbal as others.

However, it is also important to note those occasions of purposeful reticence, for each and any of us, and to consider what disinclines us from participating at that juncture.

Feedback is also an important aspect of communication in group. It is explained as a report about how one feels about the behaviour of others, extended as an offering to another member or members, or to the facilitator (more will be discussed about these kinds of communications in Chapter 31, Difficult and challenging behaviours).

It is important to explain, as has been elucidated previously, that all problems have implications for relationships, in both intimate circles and the wider social context. In addressing these issues, we can acquire some understanding of how we are experienced by others. This information can grant us a wider range of choices about how we act and respond.

Finally, in an effort to 'demystify' the role of the therapist, it is advisable to say a few words about one's own intentions and hopes. I talk about being both a participant and an observer, much like all the others in the group. I have some particular responsibilities, many of them practical, for the formation of the group. I try to dismantle any investment in me as a saviour, parent, or disciplinarian, but the proof will be in the groupwork.

## A model and rationale for time-limited structure

It has been suggested that there are pros and cons to open-ended or time-specific models: this debate is still current. Many organisations prescribe short-term contracts for counselling; this is often due to limited resources, rather than a considered way of working. More often than not, as I often hear in a supervisory capacity, practitioners are frustrated or disappointed with this arrangement.

However, I believe there is a definite case to be made for working in this manner. I would like to offer a few ideas in support of a 'brief', time-limited structure.

Much of my experience has been with ten- or twelve-week contracts. This was a format proposed by an organisation I worked with in the late 1980s. Upon resuming my studies in 1990, I realised the model reflected a number of themes and concepts central to the existential school of thought.

Again, anecdotally, the most frequent comments and attitudes that stand out in my recollection upon explaining this time-specific structure to clients were: 'Oh, it's only ten weeks, that's not enough time to really commit to any deep involvement in this group' or 'Ah, only ten weeks, I must get as much as possible out of this short time'.

One might imagine how these attitudes translate into existential concerns.

In life, we struggle with precisely these dilemmas with reference to time: procrastination, obsession with completion and deadlines, rationalisation of our goals, and the quality of our investments (both personal and professional) according to speculation on *how much time we have*.

There is no 'right' or 'wrong' about these conjectures: it's just that they are *assumptions*, and quite spurious ones at that.

In my experience, it seems that a 'short' or, in fact, any time-limited arrangement reveals, indeed *exposes*, our attitude about this most central existential issue. In contrast to therapeutic models that insist on lengthy (or at least longer) contracts, this circumscribed format more readily raises questions about commitment and efficacy; certainly, these are worthy considerations in any case. Additionally, as compared to more prolonged paradigms, 'time', too much or too little of it, is brought into focus.

The question 'what can happen in this much time?' is an existential issue: we have to make the decision as to how to 'spend' the time we *might* have. This is relative to many (if not all) of the additional ontological aspects, i.e., uncertainty, anxiety, death, relatedness, and so forth.

Such a discovery of the assumptions and conjectures by which we are living our lives can be disconcerting and also profoundly therapeutic. We are then compelled to acknowledge that we are choosing *which assumptions* are forming the basis for our choices and behaviours.

The subsequent enquiry would hopefully ensue: 'why do I need to believe in this assumption, that is, *how does it serve me, and, how does it **not**?*'

Inevitably, we are forced to make choices on limited knowledge and suppositions: the point is to discover and consider these for their effectiveness and current relevance.

There are usually quite a number of discussions around time boundaries in therapeutic endeavours. These can be a fruitful source for the recognition that the various boundaries to which we subscribe are in fact arbitrary and contingent; only those aspects designated as 'givens' (as described previously) represent the inescapable aspects of our existence, that is, those elements about which we have no choice, as in responsibility, freedom, facticity, etc.

However, the caveat persists: when we say 'yes' to something, we say 'no' to something else (and vice versa). There are pros and cons to this fixed-time model, and in the end, again, we have to choose without absolute certainty.

## Terminating the group

> Groups hate to die.
>
> (Yalom, 1995, p. 367)

Every beginning intimates an ending. The ending is not just an event: it is a process.

There is no precise way of knowing when to terminate a group, unless, of course, the ending has been set at the beginning. Otherwise, the most common rationale for the dissolution is that it seems that a few, if not a majority, of members have indicated they are prepared to do so, for a variety of reasons: they have attained a satisfactory level of understanding of their life and situation as it stands; or they wish to 'test' out their new perspectives without further reports to the group; or circumstances are such that the meetings have become inconvenient. Additionally, it may be that the therapist does not wish to continue, again, for a variety of reasons.

As the themes of temporality, death, and relatedness are central to the existential model, it is relatively easy to reference these issues during the course of the meetings. Every ending, every boundary issue, every occasion of loss, references the final one, the ultimate one, the most personal one.

The discussion here will highlight these issues with respect to time-limited and closed group situations, as these are most common, and for the sake of brevity. However, these considerations certainly have relevance for all groups, as all human endeavours change and end.

It is advisable not to insist on examination of feelings and attitudes about the ending. If this issue is pursued too fervently, too often, or too soon, it may prompt a reticence to participate, as such investment may only make the separation more difficult.

On the other hand, if this essential topic is avoided, particularly by the therapist, members may miss the opportunity to reflect on how they engage with endings in their lives in general. Their anxieties about these issues may be exacerbated if they sense that the facilitator harbours some uneasiness about the issue.

This is not to say that the facilitator shouldn't disclose their own reflections on the eventuality. In fact, such a revelation may well be just the encouragement the others need to consider and articulate their views on the matter.

I recall an instance in which I revealed that I would miss the meetings of a group that had met weekly for eighteen months. Some members of the group were a bit taken aback by my disclosure. When they admitted this surprise, I asked if they would care to say more about their experience: what was it they were so 'surprised' about? Some said they had never heard a therapist express such a personal view, and consequently I appeared somewhat less 'professional' and more 'accessible'; some reported that they were pleased at the unexpected expression of how I valued the group and asked, in return, what it was about this group that I especially prized! (It was how they rose to so many challenges, including the departure of a member without notice or explanation.) It proved to be a useful and interesting round of how our assumptions about each other had evolved.

It was also impressive to hear people engage with the exploration in a rather phenomenological manner: the 'what' and 'how' enquiries seemed to arise naturally.

In anticipating the final meeting, it is important to remind the group that they are free to construct their own ending: how do they want this to finish? How do their behaviours and feelings reflect their engagement with this issue? How does this experience compare to the endings that are or have been a part of their life external to the group? Is it 'better' to know when the ending is likely to occur, or not?

It is also imperative to note that change and growth do not stop: the effects of the experience will develop and continue.

There are also considerations that commonly appear around the approaching finality: what has changed, what hasn't, and what remains to be further explored? What were the 'turning points'? What about the group experience was 'good', and also uncomfortable? How did I (as a member) participate? How have other relationships and aspects of life been affected?

Loss, as has been proposed previously, is part of every relationship and every life situation. Change, wished for or not, brings endings and, usually, beginnings; the cycle continues indefinitely. It is apposite that all those in the group express how they experience the loss, the separation, and the 'unfinished business'.

This latter phenomenon is also an element of existence. We rarely know when this meeting will be the final one – *not everything that can be said, or 'should' be said, will be said.* It is important to consider how we deal with these interrupted relationships, particularly those situations in which an ending occurs that is not of our choosing or our intention.

It is also apposite that the facilitator expresses their sense of change and loss. I often note that I will never be the same; I too have been affected by the exchanges, and I will never *be* like I was when I was with *them*.

The termination of the group, as with so many challenges, is not something to be solved, but rather something to be worked through, from the beginning; as proposed previously, the three dimensions of time are all always present.

## References

Foulkes, S.H. *Group Analytic Psychotherapy*, 1986 (trans. E. Foulkes), Karnac, London.
Friedman, W.H. *How to Do Groups*, 1994, Jason Aronson Inc., Northvale, NJ, London.
Yalom, I. *The Theory and Practice of Group Psychotherapy*, 1995, Basic Books, New York.

# Chapter 27

# Risks, disappointments, benefits, and therapeutic effects

Risks, disappointments, benefits, and therapeutic effects *are all interlinked* and are possibilities for all those in attendance, including the therapist.

Some facilitators warn prospective members about risk factors and/or potential disappointments. These concerns are inevitably a part of the group discussion, and it appears to be more effective and emphatic if these are expressed alongside the narratives of the members: explained and demonstrated in their experiences in and of the group, and how these are similar and different to life in general.

These concerns might be broached by the candidate at the initial interview, and they should be respectfully but briefly attended to; it is apposite to acknowledge that these are not uncommon anxieties.

Themes around '**change**' – expected or not, welcome or not so much – are typical tales of how deeply this existential given affects us all. And yet, most people come to therapy with an ostensible intention to change something.

What is likely to be discovered is that change is inevitable, but uncertain and unpredictable. That which we hoped for does not satisfy us in the way we expected, and the unanticipated change, even those that we attempted to avoid, proves to be sometimes beneficial. Change is an engagement with the 'not-yet': although the desired movement may be informed by past experiences, there is no guarantee (indeed, no likelihood) that the future will mimic history.

It may be clear, then, that the longed-for modifications usually require taking some sort of risk: we cannot be certain that our aspirations will materialise when and how we wanted.

'Change' is rarely discussed in terms of one person, or only with respect to the individual reporting their experience: change will mark our inter-personal world, if not rock it. There are likely to be discussions as to how others are or might be affected by our own changes. These results may not always be satisfying; indeed, the reactions of others may be surprising, for better or worse.

It also makes sense that group members can and will be affected by the changes they experience and those that they witness: they are, after all, a part of that process.

There was a group member that aspired to becoming more 'lovable', which sprang from a complaint that his partner had often voiced; 'Jake' had hoped that the group would provide him with both understanding of his 'character' and the means by which to accomplish the desired modification. He was expecting some kind of 'exercise' or 'homework' that would allow him to 'work on' himself.

In the fifth group meeting, Jake asked permission to take a 'poll' of the members to ascertain who in the group could or would characterise him in this way. Most of the people there were cautious in their appraisal and used words like 'likeable' and 'easy' to describe how they felt about Jake; two people said they found him to be bit 'formal' and 'buttoned-up'. But none offered the precise definition that he wanted. When Jake expressed his disappointment, one of the members stated that there had been no 'loving' gesture that had come from Jake: *to 'be lovable', someone had to experience him in this way.*

The group explored this issue of how we co-create each other, 'define' each other, and how this is sometimes satisfying but, on other occasions, could be extremely distressing. Every member had something to share, some reflections on this aspect of inter-relatedness that was so significant.

It even became something of a game, along the lines of: 'In this moment I want to be . . . (trustworthy, intelligent, courageous, etc.) – how am I doing?' There was a discernible shift in how members related to each other: more accommodating, as well as more direct in expressing how they experienced each other, at any given moment. Many came to appreciate that they could play an active part in how they wished to be experienced, but this was not a total or final characterisation.

Then, there was a session in this same group in which a member related a story of how she felt she had failed her 8-year-old child, in that she could not seem to comfort him or offer any soothing wisdom when the family dog died recently, and her son was extremely distressed.

After a brief period of silence, Jake shared the story of his experience, as an 8-year-old child, of the death of the family dog ('Buster') that was acquired just after his own birth and was very much a charmed friend of his when he was so young. Jake prefaced this tale with something of an apology: 'this is something of a sentimental memory', paused, and then confided to the group that his mother had 'promised' him that the pet was in a good place with his own family members, and that he was happy there, but it was certain that 'Buster missed him too'.

Jake was visibly emotional and choked up, as he added: 'That thought, silly as it seems now, has comforted me throughout the many occasions when I still miss that dog!'

All present were still and quiet. Marion, the mother who had first spoken, thanked him for telling his story and noted: 'It is the simple and sincere sentiments that make a difference' (Marion's problem is considered further in this chapter).

This event garnered Jake the longed-for accolade: various people present recognised that this kind of deeply personal bit of history was an unusual disclosure from Jake, and they wanted him to know how much it was appreciated – not just for the content, which was affecting, but because it revealed a vulnerable side of him that had, until now, been concealed. His generosity thus acknowledged, Jake felt gratified in his quest to be seen as he had hoped to be.

Jake relayed this experience to his partner, with consent from the entire group, and she agreed that this did indeed demonstrate that 'he had it in him' and that she was pleased for and proud of him.

The episode had quite an effect on Jake, his marital relationship, and all present. As he subsequently reflected on the occasion, he recalled the anxiety that gripped him just prior to the disclosure: he felt he was about to expose a sentimental side of himself that he feared would be deemed 'unmanly' at best and a possible source of ridicule at worst.

And in spite of these concerns, *he gave something of himself because he felt he might be able to help*. This was recognised for the kindness and intention it displayed; in addition, this factor supported, and enhanced, group fellowship, sometimes referred to as *cohesion*.

Additionally, there was much discussion about risk-taking: what would be felt as risky in this group, and why, as compared to other social contexts; and what the fantasies and realities attached to those communications are that expose what we consider to be our vulnerabilities.

If this fear of exposing our shortcomings and vulnerabilities remains covert, it affects how we are in-the-world-with-others: we can become guarded, defensive, devious, and withholding. Our fears can become the basis for our behaviours and choices. Avoidance strategies become the norm.

The vignette also demonstrates, again, that we can be interpreted as others are inclined to see us, and our 'character' is relevant to how others value our choices. Additionally, every change, every choice, affects others in our milieus, and again, there is no consistency in how this is qualified.

It also illustrates that when we take a risk to disclose our anxieties and aspirations, it can result in a variety of changes: some hoped for, some unexpected, but in any case we are *different* than where we started. New challenges and changes await us. Risks, disappointments, benefits: therapeutic effects all intertwined.

For some members and applicants, it can be disquieting to have to 'share' the attentions of the facilitator, who is often viewed as the source of help and specialised knowledge. It is infrequently mentioned by those attending an orientation or intake interview; it is only when they are confronted with the reality of the situation that some semblance of disappointment sets in.

If this issue is articulated by a member, or if it is an anxiety that the therapist becomes aware of, it can be useful to flag it as a common concern that will be addressed as part of the process. It is usually more effective to address this at the first occasion when the group is working through, or has worked with, a singular issue or problem. At this juncture, it can be easily demonstrated that it is the pool of experience and understanding, the shared concerns and successes, the expanded horizon of viewpoints that are elements of the group context that can be especially therapeutic; (again) *it is in this manner that the group is the agent of change*. This principle is also adumbrated in the previous vignette.

It is frequently the case that **conflict** is considered to be a hazard of the group experience. This event will be considered in more detail in a later discussion in this text, but it can be a source of demoralisation if it is not understood for its positive effects. These are not always immediately apparent, but can and should be worked through within the group dialogues. It can also offer an opportunity to learn how to deal with unsatisfactory or unresolved relationships that, for one reason or another, are no longer available for mediation.

Members may also be wary of bearing the **'blame'** for the failure of the group as a whole or for the discomfort of some members in particular. Few of us have not been witness to, or the victim of, 'scapegoating', an event in which someone is singled out to bear the brunt of derision and responsibility for unsatisfactory circumstances.

This situation is almost inevitable, and much of the relevant literature suggests that the dissatisfaction is most likely to be aimed at the therapist. However, it can be 'dangerous' to challenge the therapist in this way (they have the power to exclude members), so a less threatening target may be chosen to bear the culpability. When any one member, including the facilitator, is singled out for such responsibility, it is an opportunity to acknowledge this phenomenon and to invite all present to consider in what way they contribute to the situation they have had a part in creating: *as no one can do nothing in a group, so it is that everyone is a part of the effects.*

The seeming inevitability of this 'blaming' scenario is due to the disinclination on the part of those involved to be held, or to feel, responsible for their own, or others', unhappiness. A meta-commentary, as illustrated previously, is apt in this situation.

There are notable therapeutic effects that are anticipated, and hoped for, and can be experienced by any participants; these can occur at various junctures in the group. However, it is important to note that, much like life, these positive, interconnected, and nuanced occurrences are not the product of linear development: they are not the consequences of predictable 'stages' of process. Yalom comments:

> There exists no empirical proof that stages in group therapy do or must exist.
>
> (Yalom, 1995, p. 303)

This accords with an earlier assertion with respect to 'time' as an existential given: the past, present, and future are concurrent, and all three dimensions impact on our memories, as well as on how we anticipate and plan for the future.

One of the most frequently reported benefits of groupwork is that of **'insight'**. This kind of realisation is one that might occur abruptly, as in a 'flash', or it may unfold gradually. There are numerous descriptions of this phenomenon, which can occur in individual therapy, certainly, but can also be a consequence of any reflective process; as suggested earlier, this event will always have an inter-subjective aspect.

In groupwork, this is most likely to reference exchanges among members: insight can provide illumination about how one is perceived by other members, and how one is at least partly responsible for this. There may be some revelation as to what values, assumptions, and aspirations are attached to inter-personal behaviour; insight reveals that there are numerous options in terms of how we engage with others.

This event is most often the result of feedback from members about their reactions to other members' disclosures, comments, or other behaviours.

As has been noted, the description is inherently inter-subjective, as is existence. The effects of such pronounced awareness and learning extend far beyond the confines of any single group context.

But the elements proposed here are also appreciated in models that are primarily intra-psychic. Patrick de Maré, a psychiatrist who promoted socio-therapy within groups of various sizes, asserts:

> 'Outsight' is a simple complementary term: whereas insight refers to inwardly oriented expansion of awareness, outsight refers to the outward expansion of social consciousness and thoughtfulness. . . . This is done through learning to talk to one another.
>
> (de Maré, 2012, p. 129)

In spite of the Cartesian implications of this view, it is apparent, even in the analytic perspective, that 'individual' processes always afford a social, inter-subjective impact.

This is another description of how inside and outside, self and other, the individual and the group are usually represented as distinct entities, instead of as conceptual conveniences. It has been asserted that such distinctions reflect parts of integrated wholes, which are different than the sum of their parts, as suggested by Gestalt psychologists, and as discussed in Chapter 2, in the review of Lewin's work.

As posited earlier in this chapter, the group is the agent of change. A primary factor in this arrangement is the condition of '**universality**': recognition that we all share the joys and tribulations associated with existential challenges. We share common ground, which allows for a fundamental understanding of what it means to be human.

We may come to understand that we are always an integral part of a wider context: *we belong to something that is different than the sum of its parts*. This realisation can to some degree assuage alienation and isolation and provide a refutation to segregation and discrimination.

We also are exposed to the reality that we are not the only ones who suffer. Our pain is owned by each of us, but in every group to which we belong, there is evidence of struggle and grief, and there are also examples of happiness and triumph. This can readily engender **comfort** and **courage**.

The disclosure that was offered by Jake to Marion about the grief of her son was an example of this kind of comfort. It was touching that Jake had made such an effort to be helpful, and it granted some tranquillity to Marion; her own distress was acknowledged and accepted. Subsequent to that exchange, she said she felt that just allowing her son to feel sorrow, being there for him, and staying with that emotional experience demonstrated a respect for his feelings and his loss: there was nothing 'to fix'.

Examples such as these foster the appreciation that self and other are inextricably bound: we can help others, and they in turn can help us – not always, not in parity, but most often, in some way, to some extent. And, we can help others by allowing them to help us. This can inspire **hope,** even if this is primarily based in the recognised possibility of being able to share and bear our burdens in the company of others.

We can comprehend that we inevitably impact on and affect others, and that these forces are reciprocal, but not necessarily in equal measure or quality: the responsibility for these effects extends indefinitely, far beyond the immediate context. This can promote **forgiveness** and **acceptance** (of the other's perspective), as our own transgressions are, sometimes at least, met with mercy.

**Emotional experience** can be appreciated for the information displayed in the values, aspirations, assumptions, and expectations implicated in every emotional response. Our world-view, mutable and dynamic, can be understood in its various aspects and appreciated as the configuration of values that inform our choices. These phenomena are welcomed in the group experience.

It is important to note that emotions are not endorsed for the sake of catharsis. The expression only launches the exploration of how we are in-the-world-with-others, and the meanings concomitant with the experience.

**Endings** are always significant, in one way or another. It is necessary to appreciate the place of mourning without succumbing to despair. Mourning, to any degree, is the expression of our care and investment over what, or who, has been lost or sacrificed. Being able to be with others in the sadness of their loss, and to have them accompany us along the same path, without faulting or pathologising each other for our manner of grief, *is all there is to do.* There is no 'solution' to sorrow; there is endurance that is supported by the kind of fellowship described here. And, as we have seen, change brings loss, and choice brings the death of some possibilities: we are in a constant web of change, loss, grief, and satisfaction.

As all human endeavours come to an end, the awareness of this inevitability can free us from the trivialities of our existence and promote a sense of gratitude for what we have and who we share it with,

The proposals with reference to risks, disappointments, benefits, and therapeutic effects of group therapy are grounded in the entire portfolio of existential givens.

It would seem, therefore, that such a view on the particulars of what might be experienced in the group setting is imminently relevant for life in general. It cannot be promised that risks will be eliminated, or that all will be well ultimately: what might be appreciated is an expanded repertoire for how to engage with these eventualities.

## References

De Maré, P. 'The Politics of Large Groups', in *Small, Large, and Median Groups*, 2012 (eds. R. Lenn and K. Stefano), p. 109, Karnac, London.
Yalom, I. *Theory and Practice of Group Psychotherapy*, 1995, Basic Books, New York.

# Chapter 28

# Focal points

## Responsibilities of the facilitator, the members, the group

The focal points addressed later are delineated in an effort to clarify a few considerations. However, it might be noted that most responsibilities and aspirations are shared among all participants. It is wise to keep in mind the proposal central to Gestalt psychology, cited previously: the whole is other than the sum of its parts. In this case, it is suggested that the group is other than the collection of individuals: it is a group – it is *this group*.

### The facilitator

The primary objective of the facilitator is to preserve the group. This is a formidable task in the face of challenging behaviours, expectations that the therapist knows the answers (but is withholding), questions about the suitability of the therapist, and inevitable disappointment with the facilitator.

The term employed here is also represented by designations of 'therapist', 'conductor' (the title preferred by Foulkes), facilitator, or counsellor. The word 'leader' obviously has connotations that might be considered a misrepresentation of the role of the therapist.

The responsibilities necessarily assigned to the facilitator are those to do with forming the group, practicalities, administration, professional ethical considerations, and logistics, as well as the arrangements for post-group assessments, should that be required. Such practicalities position the therapist as the unifying force, at least in the first instance.

It is important to consider how one's style as a facilitator reflects one's philosophy. In the existential model, this might be described as a democratic, egalitarian attitude that demonstrates that the work, for the most part, is the responsibility of the group. A more authoritarian stance, as described in the experiments reported in Chapter 2 on Kurt Lewin, requires the therapist to take a more directive role in the process. This may indicate the members are not 'trusted' with respect to their own understanding or choices; such a view is not justifiable considering the proposals with reference to existential tenets.

The role of the therapist is described eloquently by Cohn:

> The group therapist is a member of the group with a specific task – to assist in the process of clarifying the relational and communicative disturbances and potentialities of the group . . . in an existential-phenomenological group, the therapist does not 'stand out' hierarchically 'over against' the others.
>
> (Cohn, 1997, p. 55)

This proposal reflects the inter-subjective aspect of therapy (and life) and identifies the field of difficulties as the 'in-between and among', as demonstrated in communication: not only the words, but the extended field of all behaviour.

Thus, the therapist is a 'participant/observer', much like all members, but with two exceptions in terms of their involvement. The unpalatable prerogative that belongs specifically to the facilitator is that of 'dismissing' a member from the group itself: such occasions of exclusions will be discussed in further detail in Chapter 31, on difficult behaviours.

More benevolently, the therapist is singular in their relation to the group in one other specific manner:

> the conductor alone puts the group's interest first and foremost. He is in the service of the group.
>
> (Foulkes, 1986, p. 130)

It is clear that the therapist is invested in a slightly different way than other members.

There is a wealth of material about the desirable qualities of facilitators. Foulkes challenges would-be 'conductors':

> it is essential to be non-judgemental; above all, to be able to listen, and listen again; to cultivate a taste for truth, for inner honesty in the face of confrontation.
>
> (ibid., p. 109)

Foulkes also advises that the therapist be 'creative' and 'intuitive': they are immersed in the communications and conditions of the group, and the nature of their contributions will be directly relevant to what is experienced and observed in context.

However, in spite of intentions on the part of the facilitator to 'be' egalitarian, it is likely that members may have other expectations. They may hope for, or anticipate, a 'leader' who can solve their problems, assuage their suffering, or advise them on how to achieve their ambitions and aspirations.

It is, therefore, the responsibility of the therapist to be aware of these kinds of possibilities and to address them, not if, but *when* they become apparent. Any power accorded the therapist cannot and should not be exploited, accepted, deployed (even for 'good reason'), disregarded, or casually dismissed: it must be worked with. The impact of the effect the therapist will have with respect to managing the issue of their personal power cannot be underestimated. How this challenge is met will demonstrate to the members exactly what the facilitator really believes is the responsibility, and the power, of members to understand and to implement those changes to which they aspire.

On this matter, Foulkes asserts:

> If he (conductor) manages to minimise rather than support his significance . . . he will make the group into a more confident and active agent. The group will learn to rely more on itself, and be correspondingly more convinced of the truth of its findings.
>
> (ibid., p. 111)

The means by which to engage with such power dynamics (which can occasionally be focused on another member, instead of the therapist) is simply to draw attention to the assumptions being displayed and articulated. If members frequently defer to the therapist, for example, to give a first response to a difficulty or a disclosure, this can readily be noted by the therapist (and is sometimes pointed out by other members). If any one person, perhaps more heatedly, insists that the facilitator is 'the professional' and 'should have some answers', this too should be offered to the group, to consider what the implications are to such a statement. It very often comes to light that more than one member holds a similar attitude.

On one such occasion, when it became apparent to me that one member in particular was dissatisfied with what they described as my 'reticence' to give my opinion, I obliged the interlocutor with my viewpoint, stating that I thought the members were displaying a great deal of courage in attempting to come to grips with their own understandings of their dilemmas. I further commented that this was evidence that they took responsibility for their own lives quite seriously, which I respected, knowing from experience that this was not an easy process.

This was met with a short silence (in which I wondered if I had sounded defensive), and then a few members responded by saying that they appreciated the acknowledgement of their struggles and felt bolstered by the input of others about their own difficulties.

I had hoped that this comment gave some indication that I too struggled many of the same challenges they faced. I felt this was a sufficient self-disclosure for the moment, but there were subsequently similar indications that I was, to some extent, bestowed with some privileged healing power or wisdom. As with most groups, this was addressed on numerous occasions; I simply pointed out how this attitude had become prevalent and queried the implications to this line of thinking: *how did this attribution serve them? And how did it **not?***

The issue of the power invested in the facilitator is so significant that Bion proposes:

Unless a group actively disavows its leader it is, in fact, following him.
(Bion, 1961, p. 58)

As radical as this suggestion might sound, if it transpires it is at least a solid sign that the facilitator's credibility is rated on par with any other member, if only temporarily.

In terms of the anxieties, self-doubt, and vulnerabilities that might be harboured by the therapist, these are all equally possible for every member of the group. Additionally, any of the gratifying, joyful, significant, and meaningful experiences that are so often a part of the group experience are also available for the therapist. On this topic, it is important to remember that 'we are all in the same boat'.

The challenge for the facilitator is to take the same risks the others do and summon the same kind of courage expected of them in an effort to actualise the ways of being-with that can help to improve not just our own lives, but also the communal contexts of which we are a part.

## The members

The primary task for the members is to explore and reflect upon all aspects of the relationship to each member, to the leader, and to the group as a whole.

This does not mean that material about experiences external to the group should be discouraged. There is always an opportunity to compare and contrast the conditions and qualities of relationships outside the group, to explore in what ways these are the same and different and why this is so.

Neither is it advisable to insist on a 'here and now' focus. As has been discussed, any dimension of time is likely to reference another; the tales that are current will imbue previous experiences with a different shades of meaning, and also serve to shape our intentions for the future. Any of these temporal categories is ripe for exploration and reflection and will all reference current situations.

And, in much the same way as no one can do 'nothing' in a group, so too one cannot *not communicate*. All behaviours, e.g., thoughts, feelings, silences, manner of dress, and boundary infractions, are available for reflection and exploration.

Their responsibilities are to respect the agreed boundaries (and address breaches), share their experiences as truthfully as possible, notice the extent and limits of candour and disclosure (on their own part, as well as that of others), and consider the consequences and implications of any inhibitions.

## The group

The primary task of the group is to observe itself: to start with the manifest and immediate experience and seek further clarification from their own, and others', feedback. Feedback, clarification, and further reflection and feedback produce a 'loop' of dialogue and discussion, which will be discussed in greater detail in Chapter 29.

An appreciation for speaking about emotions should be fostered, and, as with any experience, these are shared with others in the expectation of an exploration of the values, aspirations, and assumptions that comprise our world-view and are revealed in our emotional responses. The means by which this enquiry can be effected was discussed in Chapters 21 and 22 on phenomenology and hermeneutics, and will be reviewed in an anecdote in Chapter 29, when we consider challenging behaviours.

The group should aspire to 'free communication' (Foulkes, 1986): free of strategy, manipulation, and deception. As argued earlier, *when this intention is avoided or denied, it is important to consider what is being chosen instead, and what purpose this alternative behaviour fulfils.* This understanding can provide a different platform for making a different choice.

On an occasion when it appears that a member is prevaricating, or just ambiguous, the therapist or another member may enquire as to what is making the communication difficult: this can refocus the exploration on the impediment, rather than on the content of the statement.

The group must transcend pure experience and apply itself to the integration of that experience: this is experiential, inter-subjective learning. There is something of a sequence to this injunction: there is an experience, a thought, an action, or an emotion, for example, and this event can be submitted to exploration and reflection with all those present in a dialogical engagement, in an effort to clarify the meanings, assumptions, and values integral to the experience. This manner of communication is expanded upon in the following chapter on the ways of dialogue. However, the point must be made that experiences, often credited for their cathartic value, are only the beginning of the process.

It is hoped the group will come to appreciate that:

> The increase in self-knowledge goes together with understanding others better; the widening of horizons is altogether profound.
>
> (Foulkes, 1986, p. 109)

## References

Bion, W.R. *Experiences in Groups*, 1961, Tavistock, London.
Cohn, H.W. *Existential Thought and Therapeutic Practice*, 1997, Sage, London.
Foulkes, S.H. *Group Analytic Psychotherapy*, 1986, Karnac, London.

# Chapter 29

# The ways of dialogue

The communication strategies to be reviewed are most effective when grounded in a way of 'bring-with'. This has been described in various ways in this text and may be recognised as a condition of 'presence'.

In presence, we allow ourselves to be open to the other in reciprocity, mutuality, attending to the other, and *willingness to be affected*. This is an important point as it differentiates these examples of communication from 'skills', which are most often applied techniques.

Bugental offers an eloquent description of this quality of 'presence':

> It calls our attention to how genuinely and completely a person is in a situation rather than standing apart from it as observer, commentator, critic, or judge . . . *presence* is a name for the quality of being in a situation or relationship in which one intends at a deep level to participate as fully as she is able.
> (Bugental, 1992, pp. 26–27, italics original)

It is significant that Bugental qualifies this notion with the stipulation 'as fully as she is able': we can recognise that we may fall short of our aspiration to be 'present'. It may be a partial or fleeting involvement, and it may sometimes be difficult to summon such profound accessibility. But acknowledgement of the inhibitions and limitations in achieving this intention can be revelatory for all parties concerned. The relationship is *co-constituted*, even in a pair, and obviously in a group: everyone contributes to the condition of the relationship(s), and the responsibility is therefore shared, even if not in equal measure. The question that arises is: how does my own participation reflect my willingness for 'being-there-with-others'?

## The first session: possibilities for facilitating communication

Anxiety will abound, for the therapist as well as the members. This is not a bad thing, but it is an occasion on which a bit of 'collusion' may be called for in the shape of assuaging these anxieties for all parties. To that end, providing a bit of structure, as opposed to the more amorphous openings for subsequent sessions, may be appropriate.

The options are numerous, but it is likely that the facilitator will be the first to speak. It is advisable to ask each member to introduce themselves in terms of how they would like to be addressed; and/or it may be an opportunity to review some procedural rules, like confidentiality.

If questions or concerns are expressed, these will probably be directed to the therapist. If there are none, it can be useful to ask members to reflect in silence for a few minutes. The therapist can then ask who would like to share how they are feeling, or what thoughts are around at that moment.

The therapist might then look around to see who might indicate they are willing to proceed and invite the person, by name, to comment. If there are no further volunteers, it can be appropriate to proceed around the circle, starting with someone seated nearby, to offer an opportunity for each person to contribute. If any members decline to comment, it should not be treated as anything unusual: this can demonstrate that different kinds of participation are permitted and in fact welcome.

This strategy has its drawbacks: the group may expect the facilitator to start every meeting. This can be quickly debunked by refraining from comment at the beginning of the subsequent session. However, this kind of structure may be advisable again in an anxiety-laden situation, for example, if a member drops out of the group permanently.

Following the initial exchanges, it is usually best to follow up with the member who discloses the most distress relevant to the current situation: this will probably encourage others to make similar revelations. Alternatively, attend to anyone who has expressed concern or difficulty in engaging with the group; this may be a practical aspect, like being late for some sessions, or an emotional one, like fear of being 'put on the spot'. Additionally, one can encourage people with a high level of enthusiasm to speak, or one may ask someone who has expressed some positive attitude to clarify how they hope that the group may help them with their problems.

If, after some work, a silence occurs that feels prolonged, it is probably best to respond to process, rather than to the content of the actual verbalisations. Such a process commentary will be discussed further, but this is essentially a very brief observation by the therapist about the general themes or activities of the group as a whole.

An example might be: 'It seems that now that everyone has had a chance to speak, a different kind of reticence is occurring; would anyone care to comment on their experience of what's happening now?'

This will serve to remind the members that they are responsible for the work: the therapist may prompt, but should be reluctant to do the work for them. If sitting in silence is their choice, then it should be respected.

In the first session, it is likely that most therapist interventions will be based on verbal content rather than the process itself. It can be useful, on this occasion, to ask members to consider, for the next meeting, what, if anything, they learned about themselves and others. Again, this is a strategy to pacify initial anxieties and is not meant to become a routine assignment.

If I feel it is appropriate, I also say that I hope we all are able and choose to return for the next session. I may issue this reminder of the contingency of our existence, and of the responsibility towards others, at junctures throughout the contract. It often becomes more noticeable when I do not make the announcement, and others comment, mostly with some wry humour, on the absence of the cue.

Ending sessions should be a simple reference to the time that has expired and, most often but not necessarily exclusively, verbalised by the facilitator. If there seems to be some concern around a member other than the therapist disbanding the group, on any occasion, it should be raised at the following meeting.

## Subsequent interactions and communications

Previously, there was some review of the principles of theory: the first being that different theories prescribe 'what to pay attention to'. In this model, what you (the therapist) pay attention to is what captures your attention: that is, any and all of it. It is most effective to commence with what is readily apparent.

**Listening** is usually the primary mode of interaction. The question must be 'what are we listening for?' In keeping with some of the principles described with reference to hermeneutics, we will be listening for what the speaker wants us to understand. This requires a 'tuning-in', an attendance to various forms of communication, both verbal and behavioural, in all their subtleties.

**Reflecting back** what one understands of the other's speech, using one's own words, is essential to an inter-personal sequence. The investment in understanding, indeed, the process of refining and *discovering* the message is the foundation for developing trust and is the essence of dialogue. This is not mimicry: this is a quality of exchange that occurs when meanings unfold.

In this exchange, there are no 'mistakes': these are simply opportunities for further thought and refinement.

Any kind of communication grounded in that quality previously described as 'presence' also evidences those conditions proposed by Foulkes (1986), in terms of talk without subterfuge. This 'dialogical attitude' might be described:

> **Dialogue** is produced in language, but it is also an *attitude* about how a conversation takes place . . . the meanings and truths of the speech are unfettered, freed from guided direction and specific intent other than understanding . . . it is spontaneous, creative, and thereby unpredictable.
>
> (Weixel-Dixon, 2017, p. 53, bold added, italics original)

And, as in presence, this dialogical attitude not only will affect those involved directly, but also is likely to impact on others who hear and witness the process.

**Feedback** is the 'backbone' of communication within group. It is something rarely employed in social contexts, but it is more often appreciated in intimate relationships (and sometimes professional, under some guidance).

Feedback is an opportunity for a person to hear how they are being experienced by someone, or some people, in their immediate context. Feedback is sourced in an honest report of the listeners' feelings and reactions to *what and/or how* the speaker is communicating.

The format for this comment is most often described as: 'When you said/did that, I felt/thought this'. This information can then be compared to the strategies employed by the speaker to achieve desired outcomes with respect to *how the speaker hoped to be experienced and understood.*

If there is disparity between the aspirations of the speaker and the interpretation of the listener, the speaker may avail themselves of alternative ways of being and communicating.

For example, if a person wishes to be regarded as 'intelligent', they may employ words or phrases that they believe will support their intention. If, however, the listener reports that they feel 'patronised', this feedback can be useful in revising the manner in which the speaker communicates, if their original intention remains. And, as noted previously, this is not a totalising or absolute definition of the speaker as a person or as a communicator.

It is also understandable for the speaker to explain that they 'didn't mean it to come out that way', or 'that isn't the effect I intended'. Such a response isn't necessarily defensive: it is a confirmed realisation. It can be appropriate to point out that the response of the listener(s) is valid and 'true', in spite of the speaker's intentions.

This is often exemplified in exchanges when one person describes another as, for example, 'controlling'. The person so defined may protest, insisting that they don't intend to be coercive, and that their intentions are something else entirely. It can be effective to point out that the characterisation is 'true', because it *is like that* for the person reporting their experience. If this is accepted as a piece of information, it can prompt clarification for all involved as to what about the behaviour or attitude is problematic.

Feedback may also be a communication regarding a mistaken assumption about what is being requested. A quite common example of this is when a speaker clarifies that they are not asking for the other to 'fix' the problem; rather, they just want, in the first instance, to be heard.

This latter exchange illustrates that 'being heard' is often enough in and of itself: this alone can change things, can change *us*.

But how do we know we have been 'heard'? If the listener can offer a reflection, a paraphrase, a response that allows us to feel or exclaim: 'Yes, that's it, that is exactly what I meant' (or something to that effect), we can enjoy some confidence that our message was understood. This kind of confirmation from the speaker to the listener also creates a gratifying bond.

To the extent that there is any trust between people, feedback is likely to affect one's own opinion of oneself. It can be demoralising to realise that the message of who and how I am is not as obvious as we might believe. With respect to the intention of the speaker to understand, if not modify, the quality of their relationships, they are more likely to be open to experimenting with novel ways of being-with-others as a consequence of genuine feedback: their repertoire of being-with is enhanced.

**Self-disclosure** is often seen as the riskiest of communications. As suggested previously, there may be concern about being judged, and therefore excluded or condemned. Additionally, if we reveal our vulnerabilities or hopes, we may be exploited. There is also some risk in being misunderstood, and remaining unaware of this.

However, it is self-disclosure, and the courage it takes to offer it, that promotes trust and intimacy; it follows that the motivation to embrace this revelation for the positive effects it often produces may become instilled.

This is true for the facilitator as well as all others. There will be times when the therapist may self-disclose to great effect, particularly when they feel there are obscure references to their role, or to the nature of their presence and contributions. Such an articulation would likely commence with a declared ownership of the feeling or view offered, e.g.: 'I feel that I am . . .'; 'I think that . . .' This could be followed by a request for feedback to the disclosure.

Self-disclosures, in conjunction with feedback, promote understanding and trust. Via this communication, it becomes apparent that we all feel vulnerable in some ways, perhaps powerful in other ways, and that we are in search of just enough safety to make us feel that we are grounded sufficiently to help others, even burdened as we are by our own frailties.

Such a quality of concordance is sometimes called '**resonance**'. We come to appreciate that we have a basis for understanding each other. As asserted previously, we all suffer, we all fear, and sometimes we can prevail with the assistance of others.

**Interpretation** is an intervention common to most psychotherapeutic models. In the existential phenomenological approach, it has a different purpose than that generally promoted by intra-psychic paradigms.

Cohn clarifies this distinction:

> Existential interpretation is not reductive. . . . It is hermeneutic, broadening the known context so that a fuller understanding of the troubling phenomena is reached.
>
> (Cohn, 2002, p. 48)

But what is 'reached' is not the conclusion: it is only a stage in an evolving understanding, which, as in hermeneutics, is infinite. As long as the search continues, new horizons of 'truth' emerge, and every new horizon presents us with another possible interpretation.

It is also noteworthy that Foulkes (1986), although referencing a different model of interpretation than described here, suggests that it is deployed on the occasions when the group is at an impasse, as that is when his help is clearly needed and when something may be lost if he doesn't intervene. If offered too frequently, or too soon, it impedes the group doing the work that belongs to them.

However, interpretations are an inherent aspect of perception and understanding and, as discussed in Chapter 21 on phenomenology, an essential part of life itself: they will therefore be an aspect of all communications by all in attendance.

Members will observe and experience the effects of all kinds of communications. They will likely come to appreciate what is effective, what kinds of **invitations to explore**, to say more, think more, assist in 'opening up' the theme, as well as prompting the speaker. They will hopefully recognise as well what may be detrimental to candour and spontaneity, as in the case of coercion.

Such explorations are bound to produce reflections on and realisations of **emotional experience**. When these are understood as the expression of values, and of the expectations and aspirations that underpin the world-view, the information and revelations of emotional experience are likely to be honoured.

**Silence**, whether experienced as a natural pause in the flow of communication or as a tactic for suppression and chastisement, can be an informative manner of being-with.

The more positive aspect of silence can be formidable and an indicator of profound understanding. Barrett offers this vignette:

> Two people are talking together. They understand each other, and they fall silent – a long silence. This silence is language: it may speak more eloquently than any words.
>
> (Barrett, 1962, p. 223)

In that interim, there is no need to explain further, to defend, or to persuade: it is an abdication of all these strategies, a concession to being-with, and 'staying-with', which leaves us speechless.

It is an opportunity that should be appreciated, demonstrated, and offered by therapists and members alike, and is likely to be, once it is experienced.

Silence as a withholding strategy can be experienced as punitive: when a response is needed or expected, the lack of verbal communication becomes a powerfully demoralising behaviour. The message often inferred from this stance is that the silent person deems the other 'unworthy' of their attention; one group member felt they had been 'disappeared' by the unexpected and prolonged silence of another member. Such an event is most usefully addressed with an enquiry to the group as a whole about how they are experiencing this situation (see 'meta-commentary' later). This redirects the focus from the reticent speaker to the group, who can then offer reflections on their own thoughts and feelings or can give feedback to the silent member as to how they are affected by the behaviour.

There is an observation of a particular nature that serves as a summary of the general condition of the group, and also as a useful communication when ruptures in trust and confidence occur among members.

The 'mass group process commentary' as espoused by Yalom (1995), or '**meta-commentary**', as outlined in various sources, is an effective means by which to 'take the temperature' of the current group situation.

Such an observation will also be an interpretation, as it is a statement about how one person perceives the current situation among group members (including the therapist): it is likely to address *how things are*, rather than the particulars of any verbal exchange. It is often a comment on the 'atmosphere' or 'mood' of the recent exchanges; it may also reference previous episodes that are somehow linked or seem apposite, which would be explained for their relevance.

An example of this might be that the facilitator notices that when particular members express their anger with others, the flow of communication quickly grinds to a halt: this observation would be delivered with brevity and without further speculation on the part of the facilitator.

This kind of remark is also common in individual therapy, for example, when a therapist articulates that the 'tone' of a particular kind of exchange seems to be disruptive and makes it difficult to retrieve the flow of thought or the level of trust usually enjoyed by both.

This process commentary can be offered by any member. Most often it is produced by the facilitator, as they are hopefully more inclined to acknowledge their own part in the impasse, if that is the case.

Any of these communications can be experienced as **challenging**. The invitation to reflect and consider, the observation from another perspective, the understanding that helps us to recognise that we are not alone in our suffering, the acceptance by others of our own view (which may be evolving even as we speak), often shifts something. When we recognise that we have chosen, and are therefore responsible, for the values that inform our behaviour, we can therefore change it or continue to choose it. These processes occur in the in-between: we act, the other responds to us, we hear it and witness it, and we may see ourselves, and our situation, differently.

This occurs in groupwork as the consequence of the group observing itself, even as events unfold.

These dialogical possibilities of communication are not as distinct as reviewed here: they merge, overlap, and are nuanced in the mix that is non-strategic communication. Trust, understanding, community, and an expansion of possibilities are likely by-products of such an attitude and such an endeavour.

## References

Barrett, W. *Irrational Man*, 1962, Anchor Books, New York.

Bugental, J.F.T. *The Art of the Psychotherapist*, 1992, Norton, New York.

Cohn, H.W. *Heidegger and the Roots of Existential Psychotherapy*, 2002, Continuum, London.

Foulkes, S.H. *Group Analytic Psychotherapy*, 1986, Karnac, London.

Weixel-Dixon, K. *Interpersonal Conflict, an Existential, Psychotherapeutic and Practical Model*, 2017, Routledge, London.

Yalom, I. *The Theory and Practice of Group Psychotherapy*, 1995, Basic Books, New York.

# Chapter 30

# An existential phenomenological model for dreamwork in group

Dreams are real. Boss describes the dream phenomenon as

> a definite mode of human existing.
>
> (Boss, 1963, p. 151)

He goes on to attest:

> Waking and dreaming are two equally autochthonous, though different pos-sibilities or modes of existing of an ever-integral and whole human being ... our existing, whether it happens waking or dreaming, reveals itself directly as a primordial being-in-the-world.
>
> (ibid.)

With this, we can understand that anything and everything we can appreciate about human existence, about human *being*, applies to our dreaming state.

As with any report, reminiscence, or experience shared by a client, we begin our exploration with the phenomenon as it presents itself: in this case, the mani-fest content of the dream.

Bracken comments:

> the dream is understood as an experience of concentrated attention and emotion.
>
> (Bracken, 2002, p. 124)

The dream is not 'abstract'. We react to the incidents we 'see' and participate in; we have emotional and visceral effects in response to the engagement. By virtue of this perspective, the significance of the dream report should not be corrupted by 'the application of an abstract model for their understanding' (Boss, 1963, p. 151).

It follows, then, that we explore the dream story in much the same way as we would any experience: we consider who was there, where it took place, what emotions, perceptions and sensations were present. The particular elements of the dream are not viewed as 'symbols' but rather are considered as they appear: a hat is a hat, an angel is an angel, a happy event is explored for its value and meaning. The phenomena are respected for their content and in their context, as they would be in any report originating from a wakeful state. But, as discussed previously, there is no conclusive understanding of any experience, and the meanings may evolve and expand.

The waking and dreaming states *reference* each other – and, upon reflection, *inform* each other. They are both incidents that demonstrate being-in-the-world for the dreamer.

We can reflect, with others, on the meaning of the dream as a whole, as well as the significations of the various elements that capture our interest or attention. In a group setting, all group members can assist with the exploration: anyone can offer thoughts and comments relevant to the narrative and to the dreamer, as they are known by the members.

It may be suggested that the dreamer tell the dream more than once, or in the present tense, and compare the results in terms of novel meanings and related experiences.

But it should be pointed out that the person who shares the dream should be in control of the process and the ultimate authority on the meaning and relevance of the dream itself. It may be apposite to 'return' the dream to the dreamer at the conclusion of the process.

There are two notable aspects to dreaming: we are often both participant and observer; the dreamer can be invited to consider what this dual perspective means for them.

There are also two aspects to the *telling* of the dream: the narrative of the dream itself and the public disclosure of the dream, which can be exposing for the dreamer. It is advisable to ask the person who shares the dream what it has been like to share it, and what it has been like to hear the comments offered about the revelation.

A group that had been together for a year seemed to favour reports of members' dreams and found this work particularly interesting and effective. Most of the members began to keep dream journals and offered their contents when they felt the dream to be especially emotive or significant.

At one meeting, a member, 'Jolie', shared something from her own journal for the first time.

She and her husband had recently purchased a large medieval property in France and were renovating the buildings. Shortly after they took possession of the house, she had a very vivid dream that she wrote about and then brought to the group.

She dreamt that she was showing the property to a small group of people with whom she was acquainted but didn't know well. After they toured the interior, she invited them to view the extensive cellars underneath the main building. She explained that there had been a few interesting discoveries of historical artefacts there, nothing of great importance, but of interest with reference to local person-alities and events.

When they descended the expansive stairway, the first thing that she noticed was the odour of damp rock and fungus. It was a smell that reminded her of the crowded cemetery directly adjacent to her family's home, where she spent a great deal of time as a child perched between headstones reading and enjoying her solitude. Jolie realised she hadn't thought of that place in years.

The cavern, which was much larger in her dream than in real life, was full of beautiful treasures that she had never seen before: there were tapestries, paintings, statuary, and ceramics that were obviously of great worth and artistry. Jolie was speechless upon witnessing this vision. She was excited and keen to inspect and show off this remarkable collection and strode boldly towards the artefacts, with her small group in tow.

But, as they neared the first small collection of paintings, which were of Christian scenarios and themes, it became apparent that the paintings were in dire condition: the paint was flaking and peeling, some had portions of the canvas missing entirely, and the picture frames, which appeared gilded and ornate, looked chipped and poorly assembled. Additionally, upon close inspection, it became obvious that these were not the great examples of fine art that they had first appeared to be.

The group, murmuring quietly, continued to follow Jolie through to view the other arrangements of artwork.

There was similar decrepitude and fakery evidenced in the chipped statues, the unravelling and shoddy tapestries, and the ornamental vases that now appeared to be poor imitations of classic design.

Jolie could hear the visitors whispering and giggling behind her: she felt shocked, embarrassed, and foolish. How could she have been so easily deceived? And why was she exposed in front of these witnesses?

At that moment, there was a rush of wind through the cavern, and the walls began to crack with a deafening noise. The group fled, with Jolie close behind, and when she emerged from the collapsing underground halls, she was alone, unscathed, with a pounding heart and weak knees – the others had disappeared.

This was when Jolie woke up from her dream.

Even as she completed telling the story, she was still agitated, flushed, and distressed.

The group was very taken by her story. There were a few brief comments about how terribly strange it had been, but oddly beautiful at the same time: it was a shared moment of gloom.

After a few moments when I felt the group had regained some equanimity, I asked Jolie what she felt at the moment, having recounted this story. She said that she again felt mystified, and a bit anxious, and that she was keen to have our help in considering what it all meant.

At this juncture, a member of the group, Shelia, volunteered that she had read a 'dream dictionary' text, and that she recalled that caves often symbolised the female sex organs, or the womb. A few other people concurred with this attribution.

I was not happy about this; it felt that the work of finding meaning had been wrested from Jolie, and that an external reference for it had somehow depersonalised the experience. I checked my response: it occurred to me that there might be, for Jolie, some value in the explication proposed, but I was hoping the exploration would find another direction. I decided to hold back on my intent to redirect the process, at least for the moment.

I needn't have worried: Jolie thanked the member for their thought, said that she too was familiar with that symbolic representation, but that it was not a 'satisfying translation'.

I decided to ask Jolie what, in this retelling, had stood out for her particularly about the dream.

She answered that it was the surprise about seeing the artworks on entering the cavern: she felt at first like she 'had won the lottery, and nobody told me!'

I was perhaps a bit keen to further her understanding, and I remarked that it sounded like a story of great fortune followed by profound disappointment and mayhem.

This seemed to strike a nerve for Jolie, but before she was able to respond, a member queried: 'what are treasures to you?' This theme was explored for a few minutes, as it turned out that Jolie's response was that 'her children' were her treasures. I was impressed with how such a simple prompt about one word yielded so much.

Another member inquired: 'What is your relationship like with your children?'

This was certainly a central theme of the dream. Jolie had indeed had very serious concerns with the situations of her two grown offspring; they were both in desperate circumstances with respect to their finances and their own marriages. Jolie was hugely disappointed with the behaviour and choices of her children, and in fact, she felt that it was to some large extent her fault, for not having instilled in them an appropriate work ethic and sense of commitment. She stated: 'perhaps I deserve to be disappointed'.

Additionally, Jolie realised that she had some anxieties about living long enough to see her offspring improve their predicament: she wanted them to flourish and have children of their own, and she wanted to be 'proud' of them.

This issue was recognised when Jolie remarked on the pungent odours that met her at the entrance to the vault, and that she connected to her own childhood pursuits. She had been a happy youngster and had the loving attention of her parents, with whom she had a deep, life-long connection, until their death. She wondered aloud if she would ever share such a relationship with her own children.

After some exploration among all the members of this theme of responsibility, especially with respect to children and family, there was a restful pause, where it felt that we reflected together and gathered our thoughts. Many had shared their own difficulties with family issues and how they were being dealt with and endured. Unusually, there was little in the way of outright advice. It was not a discussion in search of a resolution; the main pursuit was the deeper appreciation of each other's experiences, setbacks, and hopes.

At some point, a group member commented: 'I also find it interesting that the paintings had a religious theme: as I understood from your comments here in the group, you don't hold particularly religious beliefs; I recall you proposing that "everything happens for a reason"'.

The exploration that ensued was a memorable example of what I understand to be a real dialogical engagement: the questions posed were related to the answers given, which in turn posed further routes of reflection and enquiry.

Jolie realised that her view, as correctly summarised previously, did not 'line up' with her proposal that she alone was responsible for the predicaments of her family members. She did retain her belief that 'everything happens for a reason' – but how then *could* she be ultimately responsible for other people's situation, for better or for worse? There was some other force at work that had a part in the events besetting her family.

She, and others, considered the responsibility that each of us bears in our own lives. Of course, it was also noted that this responsibility is concomitant with our freedom, and this too is a blessing and a burden. What was difficult to understand was exactly what their responsibility was in terms of their own problems, or fortunes; it was impossible to qualify what was 'deserved' and what wasn't.

In a subsequent session, Jolie also made a connection with this dream in terms of the people she had been with: they bore a striking similarity, in terms of being 'acquaintances' she didn't know well, to the present group. She was sometimes satisfied with their input and company, but she was also sometimes wary of disclosing something that would draw ridicule, or of making a comment that would provoke abandonment (which is what happened in the dream). She also mused about the murmurings of the small crowd in her dream: she couldn't 'quite understand' what they were saying, but she was aware that it was criticism directed towards her. This too was a worry with reference to the group and to her wider social circles as well.

Trusting others in most situations was a difficult leap for her, but she added that this concern had been greatly assuaged by the developing bond taking place in the group. This opened up conversations around how trust is engendered, how it can be broken, and sometimes how it may be recovered.

This exploration, which took place over a few sessions, provided some insight into Jolie's then-current world-view: she often felt personally responsible for the predicaments of those closest to her. She was somewhat cynical about other people's trustworthiness and acceptance. The world was a mysterious and too often dangerous place; the cosmos was governed by a covert and purposeful ('but not necessarily rational') agenda.

The themes that emerged referenced a number of existential issues: 'death', of hopes and expectations; 'responsibility', and how it impacted her relationships; 'time' running out for realising significant aspirations, and the concomitant 'anxiety' associated with this possibility; the intention and aspiration for particular 'change', as well as fears of the final event; 'meaning', in terms of her closest relationships to her family; and relatedness, with reference to her anxieties about how other people 'saw' her.

As is common with dreamwork, there were elements of the dream that were revisited, retold, reconsidered: even as this took place, Jolie's world-view came into focus, and adaptations were made where it was discovered that some assumptions and values were contradictory, or not in accordance with her intentions. Changes were actualised, sometimes immediately, sometimes with prolonged consideration for what consequences *might* ensue.

Dreams are as credible a source for understanding our ways of being-in-the-world as any other experience. It would be a pity to lose the valuable information they can reveal, and exploring them in the context of our 'with-world' offers the opportunity to further clarify how we live and relate.

## References

Boss, M. 'Daseinanalytic Approach', in *Psychoanalysis and Daseinanalysis*, 1963 (ed. L.E. Lefebre), p. 151, Basic Books, New York.

Bracken, P. *Trauma, Culture, Meaning and Philosophy*, 2002, Whurr Publishing Ltd., London, UK, Philadelphia, USA.

# Chapter 31

# Difficult and challenging behaviours

As has been noted, human beings are not entities the way a brick or a flower is a 'thing' with a readily identifiable essence. Humans are 'existing', standing out from all else in a process that lasts a lifetime: we are complete only after death. It is, therefore, a fallacy to definitively assign a characterisation to a person: there is always the possibility of a variance in their choices and behaviour.

It should also be recalled that all behaviour is purposeful. We choose action in light of our world-view, and these choices are aligned with the values, aspirations, expectations, and assumptions reflected in that paradigm.

This chapter will offer descriptions of what are sometimes recognised as 'difficult' or 'challenging' behaviours. Although these behaviours are demonstrated by individuals, it would be inappropriate to identify anyone with a particular title related to behaviour, as in a 'bully', a 'coward', or even, perhaps, a 'saint'. It can be humbling to recognise that any of us may be experienced by others in ways we ourselves might not recognise; and that we may be described as a particular kind of character that references events or incidents that were witnessed, but in which, according to ourselves, our intentions were 'misunderstood' by onlookers. As proposed previously, it is exactly this prerogative that is unnerving: others are at liberty to describe us as they see fit.

What most of these strategies, these behaviours, have in common is that they are deployed in an effort to gain some benefit or advantage with respect to relatedness. This may be to conceal vulnerabilities, to garner support or collaboration, to influence or coerce, and, most definitely, to control the proximity and/or distance of others, that is, the degree of intimacy.

The stereotypical strategies listed here will be described with reference to these concerns.

There are those that seek to monopolise the conversations: they have a need to be 'centre stage' and can readily turn any topic into a narrative about their own concerns. This may also include a bid to be 'special' by insisting that their difficulties, or successes, are incomparable. This latter proposal also serves as a premise for rejecting the help offered by members: nothing compares, therefore anyone's advice or contribution is irrelevant. In this manner, they maintain a 'special' if not superior status, or so they believe: others are relegated, as they 'cannot possibly understand'. They wish to engender sympathy but refuse to demonstrate any 'need' for anyone else.

A sense of control over others is also achieved by 'holding the floor'. Others may be too polite or too intimidated to interrupt; the speaker avoids challenge or confrontation by filling the space. In such a situation, the speaker also controls how much is demanded of them in terms of genuine self-disclosure, either in offering it or hearing it.

Then there may be those who are unable, or disinclined, to offer an appropriately empathic or sympathetic response: they would prefer not to get 'too involved', as it may be discovered that they have little or nothing to offer in terms of aid. They would themselves be rendered 'useless' by those needing or seeking help.

Individuals who believe that they are special in their suffering are often those that are also too self-absorbed to recognise an appropriate level of self-disclosure. This situation most frequently occurs at the first session, or at least in an early meeting: a member offers a personal revelation that is something of an 'over-reach' or an over-sharing.

This was dramatically demonstrated in a group I was facilitating for parents who had, at some point, all lost a child. Five minutes into the first meeting, one of the parents, 'Sian', revealed that she had a neurological condition that would probably render her severely disabled in the not too distant future. She further commented that she had little faith that her spouse had the capabilities necessary for caring for herself and her surviving two children. This announcement was delivered dispassionately, and in a raised voice.

One member of the group responded almost immediately and offered to assist in the care of the family and with practical household chores, should these activities become impossible for the speaker to manage. Subsequent to this interaction, the group fell silent for a good eight minutes.

I asked Sian how she felt, at this moment, considering the silence that followed her disclosure. She apologised for making everyone uncomfortable, but said that she felt it important that the others understood the extent of her difficulties. I thanked her for sharing what was obviously a highly painful and emotional situation. After a brief pause, I asked if anyone else would care to explore how they were affected by the current ambience among us, without necessarily addressing the particulars of the speaker's circumstances. I also reminded those present that the value of feedback had been raised at the intake interviews.

Many of the reactions were directed specifically to Sian. Initially, there were queries about what she hoped for from this disclosure; there was also some 'blaming' for how some members were impacted. Equally, there were more sympathetic comments from people who said they too harboured concerns about failing to 'be there' for their own family members. One parent said that she felt her grieving was sometimes 'self-indulgent', and she had failed to notice the sufferings of those around her. Sian was taken aback at these comments and admitted the responses were not what she expected. She declined at this point to say anything more.

Such an ill-timed disclosure often has the effect of 'protecting' the speaker from further enquiries. The 'big reveal' was over and done with; it felt to me, and to others as well, that the message was that no further disclosure should be expected of this member.

I communicated this latter view to Sian, in a feedback format that eventually became appreciated: 'When you made your announcement, I felt you were demanding something of me, and us. I think it was sympathy that you wanted, and indeed, that is something I believe we all do feel, but I also felt you were warning us not to probe for anything more'.

I was worried that it might be too soon to issue such a response, and indeed, this was met with a tense silence from the group as a whole, until someone volunteered that this correlated with their own experience of Sian's communication; a few others confirmed they had similar impressions.

I added that Sian could reply to this feedback, if she wished, but she would not be pushed to say anything if she didn't want to. She maintained her silence but did become an active participant in the subsequent exchanges.

The discussion that commenced that afternoon continued throughout the twelve weeks we met. The early revelation had silenced some members: they didn't know how to respond, and they felt their own problems couldn't possibly warrant the consideration awarded to the situation that was shared. Others felt angry that this had been broached so early, and they felt equally uneasy about their irritable response: they felt that all other problems had been 'upstaged', and that the speaker had forcefully positioned themselves as the one most deserving of concern and attention. As a consequence of this event, some of the members 'retired' at first, but eventually shared reflections on their various and developing reactions.

The anxieties aroused by the event were discussed as part and parcel of the issue of 'hostile honesty'. Genuine disclosures were welcomed, and appreciated, but it also became apparent that a certain level of sensitivity for the possible impact of feedback and disclosure was as important as the freedom to express oneself. It was more effective to respectfully consider the timing and circumstances of revelations (although one could still get it wrong). This signalled the development of group cohesion: *everyone mattered*, which is essential for inter-subjective responsibility and therapeutic effects.

It is seemingly more effective, at these junctures where the entire group is affected by the communication of one person, to offer a 'meta-commentary' (as in the earlier example) that addresses the group as a whole and is concomitant with an invitation for anyone to speak, if they wish. This puts the responsibility for the process back to the group and may also serve to shift the onus from the original speaker.

The purpose of such an intervention is to encourage feedback that will assist the speaker, and all those present, to consider, if not *discover*, how their manner of communication affects others' views of them. This effect will also impact how the members feel about themselves-in-relation. This generalised description of what seems to be happening in the group may be contested by some members if they feel they are not well represented by the comment: this is simply grist for the mill.

Frequently in group therapy there is a consistently silent member; they may be exercising their prerogative of privacy, but it is often experienced as 'withholding' or seen as a protective measure that precludes deeper participation. In many instances, other members express that they feel it is a hostile position. Such a member may be invited to comment on any given topic, even that of their own reticence. The silent member may indeed be getting something out of the proceedings, but others become resentful, and suspicious, of someone who refuses to share themselves and declines to take the same risks they do.

The quiet member may indeed be shielding themselves from being probed for disclosure, but their defensive strategy deprives themselves, and others, of the safety and trust that is the product of engaging with shared vulnerabilities. This is sometimes clarified in the discussions carried out by members who may opt for talking *about* the silent member in their presence: a disingenuous way of delivering feedback.

Such a tactic usually has the effect of drawing the reticent member into the discussion, if only in defence. This is not necessarily a negative beginning, although it may be an awkward or heated initiation.

If the silent member is staunch in their refusal to participate verbally, they may be in danger of being targeted for the role of 'scapegoat'. This is an exercise by the group, or a few members, to place the responsibility for the group difficulties on one person, other than the facilitator.

When I started working with groups in a professional setting, I used to state that one behaviour in which I would definitely intervene would be scapegoating. Then, in an early session of a newly formed group, a member contested my position by stating that they 'enjoyed' being the scapegoat. The group members found this so intriguing that they worked the issue with the speaker making the claim, and very responsibly and effectively considered their own concerns about this assertion and how it affected the entire group.

Many of them pointed out that if a member aspired to the role of scapegoat, it rendered the others as persecutory characters: this arrangement was not welcomed.

When a member of the group asked 'why' the scapegoat position was desirable, the person who spoke of their intention stated that he liked 'to stir things up' and would be bored if things were 'quiet for too long'. The group continued to discuss how this proposal impacted them. Most people were somewhat amused by the notion that the 'scapegoat' position could be an attempt to control the proceedings.

This was a most valuable lesson for me: as the group is the agent of change, it is, to some great extent, their responsibility to engage with challenging behaviours. If they suffer the controlling strategies of any member, then they co-constitute the problems that their tolerance effects. Such acquiescence is likely to be problematic in other arenas of relationship when dealing with manipulation and denigration.

And, as it became clear to me, problematic behaviour is a situation that belongs to the whole group.

Strategies of monopolising, over-sharing, recalcitrant silence, help-rejecting sharing, trivialising or superficial reporting, and self-victimisation are not so distinct in actuality. These tactics can be deployed in a variety of nuanced combinations, and by anyone. If we don't feel safe in any relational situation, any of us can and will adopt some kind of strategy until we do feel 'safe enough'.

In terms of how the therapist, and members, can engage with these manoeuvres, it is important to appreciate that the point of therapeutic work is to help people better understand their choices and behaviours *via feedback from others, which helps in the recognition of how their chosen strategies serve them, and at what cost.*

Feedback, as discussed earlier, is best when it is offered as a report on how one person experiences another's behaviours and communications. It is much less effective if it is presented as an analysis of motivation or intention (as in, 'I think you're behaving that way because you had a bad childhood'). This exchange should be modelled by the facilitator, who should be transparent about the manner and effects of the feedback loop. Subsequently, it is usually carries more impact if the feedback originates with the members.

## Conflict

Conflict may not be employed as a strategy, but it is inevitable in relationships and situations *that matter to us*. If what we value is impeded or threatened, we respond in anger and employ whatever defence we deem necessary. Thus, it can be understood that *anger is a response to a pending, past, or possible loss*. Once this is addressed, by removal, relegation, or mitigation of the threat, other emotions, values, and intentions come into focus.

This proposal supports the assertion made in one of my previous publications: conflict is always personal (Weixel-Dixon, 2017).

If members of a group *care* about the group, themselves, and each other, conflict is ineluctable: at some point, the interests of others will likely impede our own.

It is hoped that facilitators will not attempt to divert, diminish, or disapprove of conflict: it presents opportunities to clarify what we value about any given event or relationship. If I am happy, I am pleased about some value being realised; if I am irritated, I am concerned about some aspiration or expectation being thwarted.

The explorations as to 'what makes you pleased/concerned/threatened about what was said, what was done, what was suggested' are the lines of enquiry that can serve to reveal (sometimes with unexpected results) what values are implicated in any given situation. It is necessary to understand what is at stake before resolutions can be considered.

Conflict also signals the possibility of change: primarily, gain or loss. However, even if the status quo is restored, the threat has been recognised, and safety has been compromised.

And it is change that the working through of conflictual situations can effect, often in ways that might not have been imagined otherwise.

This result is produced by the sharing and airing of seemingly opposed perspectives. At first we defend against loss; then, if we can hear the other perspectives, we may discover opportunities for cooperation and means of support in implementing intentions: ways forward that were previously obscured.

If one vanquishes, the contributions and participation of others is sacrificed. In the grandest philosophical, sociological sense, this is why we need each other: we cannot do it all on our own.

Conflict in the group is likely to be cyclical: less at the beginning, more as the group establishes trust. It is a revelatory experience to appreciate that conflict need not be destructive; in fact, when a difficult exchange is worked through, it can create as firm a bond as any more pleasurable event.

In an all-women group that I facilitated, I had two members who were frequently irritable or impatient with one another. Sonam was somewhat reticent, whereas Alia was loquacious and excitable. The source of the aggravation appeared to be that Alia was ignorant, or purposefully defiant, of Sonam's attempts to discredit Alia's insistence on the similarities of their background and perspectives: both women were of Indian origin.

Initially, Sonam would be polite in stating that she did not share Alia's views, about almost everything; but her patience wore thin, and her rebuttals to Alia's imposed alliance became more heated.

Finally, Sonam angrily rebuked Alia for asserting, to the group, that as they shared cultural origins, they 'most assuredly' held the same views about homosexuality.

Sonam adamantly stated that Alia had 'no idea' what she herself thought about homosexuality, and that she resented being characterised as someone who 'bought in' to commonly shared attitudes attributed to Indian women. Sonam further stated that she found it inappropriate and 'extremely' presumptuous that Alia asserted such affinity. 'Who do you think you are?' demanded Sonam: 'and who do you think *I am*? How dare you misrepresent who and how I am to these people – I will not put up with this anymore!'

Though the group had been together for eight weeks (of a twelve-week contract), there had been little evidence of disagreements among the members. I thought that some members had been aware of the growing tension between Sonam and Alia, but no one had commented on the situation.

With this outburst, everyone was instantly attentive.

At this juncture, it didn't feel as though there was going to be much more of an exchange: Alia was sitting with arms crossed, eyes lowered to the floor. Sonam was also sitting with arms crossed, and her anger seemed to heat the room.

I felt that this was a highly charged situation, so I took it upon myself to ask for clarification. I asked Sonam what it was 'that so infuriated her about Alia's assertions'; I hoped the use of 'infuriated' would let her know that I understood how deeply affected she was.

Sonam turned to me and said: 'Well, wouldn't you be? I could easily point out that you Americans all display an attitude of entitlement: you are well off, and think that your circumstances demonstrate your superiority'. After a brief pause, she continued: 'How do you like being defined by your culture, and the assumptions that are attached to that?'

As a matter of fact, that comment did strike a nerve: I had been in Europe for more than thirty years, and felt more affinity for this culture than that of my origins. In that moment, I realised that I was proud of my adaptation, and I did, in fact, bristle at the accusation. I put this realisation aside for review later and considered what might happen next: would the group engage with these themes of identity?

Before anyone could say anything else, Alia demanded in a strident voice: 'Why do you need to deny your own culture?' Sonam replied with equal force: 'Why do you need to believe that I am like you?'

This felt like a significant moment: both women had asked for further explanation. This was a good place to start unravelling the values and assumptions implicated in this contretemps.

On the back of the questions posed, I suggested that we begin by each of us offering, if we wished to, how we hoped to be experienced by the group, and how we felt thwarted or supported in this aspiration.

It became clear that Sonam felt that she had been reduced to a 'stereotype' by virtue of Alia's insistence that they shared a culture and therefore a particular world-view: she was keen to be seen as a forward-thinking individual who had developed her own perspectives on the world. Sonam wanted to 'stand out', be seen as 'unique', and she felt this was a very meaningful purpose.

It was also clarified that Alia felt that she didn't really 'fit in' with the group, who, apart from me, were all of European origin. The women in the group were all employed, and most did have children, but Alia and Sonam did not have the financial need to establish a profession, nor were either of them interested in doing so. Alia was hoping to find an 'ally' in Sonam, and support for her own world-view, which seemed to be out of sync with most of the other women. Alia commented that she wished to be experienced as a kind and generous person, who tried hard to make sure others felt accepted and supported. Alia wanted to 'be a part of' something meaningful and communal; she felt the entire universe was interconnected in this sense.

The discussions that followed concerned what it was like to try to be 'seen' as we wished to be, and what it was like when someone characterised us in a manner that we found unacceptable. On either occasion, it was an experience that was more often frustrating, if not downright demoralising, than it was gratifying. The power of others to see us in ways that may seem totally foreign to us was, once again, the principal concern.

Additionally, the world-views demonstrated in the values expressed by Sonam and Alia became intelligible: aspirations for oneself (unique, or alongside others), expectations of others and how they should 'be' (helpful, supportive), the view on the world context (belonging, difference, cooperation), and the perspective on the cosmos (one plays a part in one's destiny; one includes the entire universe in one's choices).

This group had four weeks remaining in their contract: working through this difficulty engendered a strong sense of being-with. Communication became more fluid, less guarded. The ending was honoured over the last sessions; members articulated their gratitude, both to individuals and to the group, for the whole-hearted participation that proved to be a therapeutic context for challenges and changes.

## Walkouts, drop-outs

If a member walks out of a group meeting, it is usually best if the therapist excuses themselves and follows the person once they have actually exited the room. This needs to be done with some alacrity, as the point is to catch the member before they leave the building or the premises.

It is best if it is the facilitator takes this action. If another member were to follow, it may occasion an incident of sub-grouping, even if it is only a pair. Even if this is not an intended pairing, it may be viewed with some concern by others: they may feel guilty or awkward about not having volunteered to accompany the person who has exited, or may feel excluded if no massage is relayed by the member who returns to the room.

Outside of the meeting room, the member who is proposing to depart should be encouraged to return, once they have composed themselves; they should not be made to feel that they have committed any great offence. If they decide to depart, the therapist should ask specifically what message they are allowed to convey to the group: if there is no message agreed, this in itself should be communicated to the group.

The person who has walked out may wish to re-enter with the therapist, or take a brief recess before they return. If it is at all possible, the group should be notified as to whether or not the member will return for another session.

When the therapist returns to the group, they can deliver the message and/or explain that the member will or will not return for this session, or any other statement that the departed member wished to convey.

The facilitator should immediately invite the group to share their thoughts and feelings about the event. It may be that there is no definitive answer as to whether the member will return or not.

Such occasions are common and should be treated respectfully, but not critically. Everyone in attendance is there voluntarily and is at liberty to depart at any time. This makes it all the more significant that all that show up for the meetings *do so out of choice*, a fact which renders their presence all that more valuable.

Drop-outs are voluntary recusals: the member decides that the group is not fulfilling their needs and/or expectations and does not wish to 'work through' their concerns.

Drop-outs can be a product of inadequate preparation or information about the process before the sessions commence. However, this rationale is difficult to qualify and may be an explanation that allows the exiting member to avoid their share of the responsibility for the quality of the group. The most common reason given is that they do not feel they 'fit in', and that the purpose of the group holds little relevance for their personal difficulties.

The member that withdraws may or may not give notice or reasons for their departure: they may send a message to the group via the facilitator, when and if they have an exit interview. The best-case scenario is one in which the member agrees to voice their reasons for leaving in a group meeting: unfortunately, this occurs infrequently. The therapist should attempt to arrange a private meeting with the departing member to grant them an opportunity to explain their choice, and to clarify what message, if any, they wish to convey to their fellow members.

The group may possibly feel some responsibility for the withdrawal, or question the values of the group, or believe the therapist made some faux pas that prompted the person to decamp. It seems that regardless of the explanations produced or offered, there is likely to be some uncertainty about the actual basis for the departure.

## Exclusions

Involuntary exclusions are more problematic but nonetheless sometimes necessary. There is no 'graceful' way to manage this action; it is likely to be difficult for all in any case.

If a member is continually obstructive, or not working effectively despite feedback and invitations from the group, then it is incumbent upon the facilitator to protect the interests of the group by requesting the member discontinue with the group.

It is likely, in such scenarios, that the member having and creating difficulties would not benefit from continuing their membership; neither are they likely to make useful contributions to the group.

The facilitator should conduct an 'exit' interview in private with the member concerned. The excluded person should be encouraged to seek individual therapy or to entertain the possibility that this group was not right for them, for any number of reasons (some of which they will themselves volunteer). The content of this meeting should be kept confidential, apart from what disclosure might be agreed.

The group, when informed of the action taken, is likely to have a number of strong reactions: it can be understood that some will fear that they could 'be next'. Some members may believe that the therapist abandoned or rejected the person for their own reasons; or, preferably, that the facilitator did what was necessary to preserve the cohesion of the group. The facilitator should offer a succinct explanation that indicates they chose to act in what they considered to be the best interests of the group.

In either of the latter two situations, members should not be encouraged to contact the departed member: it can result in a form of sub-grouping that remains external or indiscernible to the group, and it may be an unwelcome gesture that would exacerbate the former member's discomfort.

Behaviours that are disturbing or even disruptive of group cohesion should be challenged at the earliest possible opportunity: it is always possible that exploration of the events can be therapeutic, or at least helpful in clarifying intentions.

## Reference

Weixel-Dixon, K. *Interpersonal Conflict, an Existential, Psychotherapeutic and Practical Model*, 2017, Routledge, London, UK.

# Chapter 32

# The ambiguity of ethics (with apologies to Simone De Beauvoir)

Ethics often refers to guidelines surrounding practicalities. Such information abounds in readily available psychotherapeutic literature, and I hope it would be consulted by practitioners with reference to their own professional organisations, if they have such affiliations.

All ethical models provide a basis for the evaluation of behaviour: these are public proposals that reference social and cultural values. However, such evaluations are not absolute or definitive: as behaviour is a choice, it demonstrates the qualities of that existential aspect.

This chapter will focus on what it means to assume an ethical stance, that is, *to be ethical*. To this end, we will review some philosophical principles that may serve to illuminate the nature of this attitude.

De Beauvoir proposes:

> One does not offer ethics to a God.
>
> (De Beauvoir, 1948, p. 10)

'God' does not suffer the dilemma of *choice*: all options are available; failure is not possible.

The significance of this proposal is profound. Because we can – in fact, must – *choose*, with limited knowledge, in all uncertainty of the outcome, we need, *require*, some parameters, even if they are the product of an imperfect being. Otherwise, we can drown in the infinite sea of possibilities.

This also presupposes that we have the freedom to choose, as has been discussed in this text. This does not imply that all options are open to us: the greatest latitude in our exercise of agency is in adopting an attitude towards those aspects of our existence that we do not choose.

But we can choose to abide by 'rules', or flaunt them, or adapt them to our own views: this is the essence of freedom. If such liberties were not available, we would have no basis on which to evaluate anyone's behaviour; we would simply be automatons without recourse to do anything differently.

We will fail in our intentions to be 'true' to our ethical standards, inevitably: they are ambiguous generalisations. We notice quite readily that they often don't reference *me, in this situation, at this time.*

Every ethical dilemma demonstrates that the difficulty lies in the fact that not all ethical values, or standards, can always (or in fact rarely) be satisfied in any given challenge. We realise early on that some standards will be sacrificed in the actualisation of others.

So how do we then choose *which ones to relegate?*

Commenting on the general principles of ethics, Warnock remarks:

> it is . . . largely a matter of judgement and decision, of reasoning and sentiment, of having the right feeling at the right time.
>
> (Warnock, 1998, p. 7)

As each person is free to choose what to value, it may seem that by choosing anything, it becomes 'right' or 'correct' or 'ethical' simply by virtue of having chosen it. If this is the case, then nihilism reigns and, it might seem, 'anything goes'. But, as has been proposed in this text, we abide in a 'with-world': our fates and futures inextricably bound.

As proposed by Sartre (1973), when we choose, we choose for everyone. We bear the responsibility for our choices and also how they affect others, perhaps even infinitely. Additionally, our choice *is ourselves,* and this impacts our shared world. The choice we make as to *how to be* can be adopted and justified by anyone else who cares to follow our path, because we chose it to be the 'good' option (not necessarily moral, but in the service of our intentions).

With respect to this communal accountability, the following proposals support an ethical position and a rationale for ethical decision-making that can and should be offered in a public context.

When considering an action or decision, it is important to bear in mind the possible consequences, for everyone who might be affected, of the measures under review. This also implies that the communal and cultural contexts are taken into consideration.

It is also incumbent upon the decision maker(s) to offer an explanation for the thought processes that effected the decision.

The premises thus arrived at must be freely adopted, without subordination to legal, professional, or other external authorities.

The kind of questions these considerations raise with respect to therapy of any kind are: do we know what the risks and benefits are, for the individual and society, in engaging in this process? How do we evaluate whether we are capable of delivering the results we promote? How do we justify our way of working? What is the basis for the monetary fees?

These queries represent just a few of the ethical challenges apposite to our therapeutic endeavours. In a response similar to that required for an authentic engagement, we can be resolute; we can anticipate such opportunities to wrestle with possible failures, inadequacies, and dissatisfactions.

An example of such an ethical dilemma arose when I was asked to facilitate a group of recently qualified business coaches who wanted to have some experience of groupwork. They did not want a 'training seminar'; they were looking for an experience that was 'closer to the real thing'. Although the situation was unusual in its professional composition, and a number of them knew each other, I decided that it was a good opportunity to promote this format. We contracted for ten weekly sessions. I did not conduct intake interviews: I felt that this was unnecessary, considering the common interests already shared among the members. Additionally, they had been referred to me by a colleague who had worked with them previously as a trainee group.

I did send out a written contract that briefly outlined practicalities and provided a succinct description of the inter-relational basis of the work.

Introductions went smoothly at the first meeting. There was one member who was five minutes late, 'Steve', but he offered no apology or excuse. He said 'hello' and nodded to the members seated next to the empty chair that was waiting for him. I asked him to introduce himself, briefly, and he gave his name and noted that he knew everyone there from a previous training group.

Before anyone could say anything else, Steve moved his chair, noisily scraping it across the uneven tiles. He moved it again twice, each time just a few centimetres, but he was then seated slightly outside the tidy circle of chairs that I had arranged for the session.

I asked if he was comfortable there; before he could reply, a member directed a comment to Steve: 'It already looks like you don't really want to be a part of this!' Steve grinned, tilted back in the chair, and then let it slam back to the floor.

'Yes, I am ready to go', he replied.

His positioning left him 'half-in' and 'half-out'. His posture, his use of the space and the furniture, was already off-putting: nothing amicable about his entrance, he was prepared for a contest.

I was already wary of him: his behaviour seemed defiant, and I suspected I would be the target of his complaints at some point. I could tell there was some tension, but I decided to wait and see what would happen.

In this session, Steve spoke quite a bit about his discontent with the quality of the teaching at the college where they had all studied: the faculty didn't 'know what they were doing', 'could not explain their methods', and generally 'infantilised' the students. He was articulate and adamant about his critique.

There were differing opinions on the topic; some students stated that they had few concerns on this aspect of the training, but these opinions came from a small coterie of those present. The conversation seemed to me to be somewhat stilted, but I assumed it was a product of first-session anxieties. The chatter finally ground to halt.

At this point, Steve addressed me, and asked me to comment on what he considered to be a 'transference' situation within the group, with reference to myself: he proposed that the members were too 'deferential to you to speak their own minds'.

Admittedly, I was inclined to ask him how it was that he obviously did not suffer from this same inhibition, but I knew the issue at hand was a question about my competence and power.

I decided to specifically address the competence issue first, as I suspected there was some curiosity about me, and how I worked, among the members; this was common. I simply stated that 'transference' wasn't a phenomenon that was recognised in the way I worked, but we could certainly discuss how the quality of our relationships might be impacting the communications.

It sounded a bit long-winded, as it came out, but it prompted some engagement. Not surprisingly, the first to respond was Steve.

'If you don't work with transference, what do you do? It already sounds mysterious'.

By 'mysterious', I think he meant 'suspect'.

I weighed my answer carefully: 'We can reflect on and explore how we are together, with each other, and how our relationships – that is, any of them – affect us, our existence, and the other people in our lives'.

It seemed this satisfied some, but not others.

'But what are *you* here for – what can you do to make our lives any better?' Steve was again the first to probe.

To which I responded: 'I hope I can assist you in discovering how *you* can make your lives better – and consider what other kinds of possibilities there are for you. In fact, this is an objective that will require the participation in kind of everyone here'.

One of the other members picked up on this comment and suggested that the attitude I had described made it clear to her that I wasn't there to 'lead', in the sense that I would be directive; she understood it as 'facilitate', which was a notion with which she was familiar in her own work.

This seemed to break the ice, somewhat, at least in the sense that Steve ceased to monopolise the conversation, and some of the others spoke up for the first time.

However, Steve frequently queried me directly about how I worked and was never really satisfied with my succinct answers. I found this interrogation irritating (it was awkward to reply in brief), but felt bound to offer some reply. I felt it was important for others who might also be sitting with similar curiosity, and it was also something of an ethical obligation to offer a rationale for the purpose and manner of the therapeutic project.

I was also aware of feeling that I needed to 'prove' something: could I simply articulate my position, or was I trying to persuade them that I held a 'credible' view? I was cautious, however, of the discussions becoming about theory, which could distract from the inter-personal work.

In the next two sessions that followed, Steve was the first to speak. The beginnings always felt stifled, burdensome; it always took some time for the others to free themselves from the tyranny of Steve's continual diatribes about 'professionals' and the ineptitude of others. It was apparent that he was just not interested in hearing from anyone else and, certainly, either couldn't or wouldn't engage in any invitation to reflect on his own participation, including in this group.

Noticeably, no one volunteered any feedback to Steve. I felt it was expected that I would be the first to offer such input, but I thought it would be better coming from group members: they were probably more threatened by him than I, and it would be more effective if it originated with those who knew him better and had endured it longer.

I wondered what he was defending against with this strategy. Was he unable, or unwilling, or both, to consider how he might be experienced by the others in the group, or in his personal and professional life? I speculated on how this behaviour served him, and at what cost.

He spoke almost non-stop: it effectively held the others at arm's length. I mused silently it seemed that in lieu of relating, he 'did' talking. It was a very limited, shallow way of being in the midst of others, without being with others in any reciprocal engagement.

However, the other members did follow through with some feedback to each other and self-disclosures about themselves that reflected a developing trust. Steve did not seem to be interested in these exchanges and became quiet in those moments when others were most verbally active, although his bored yawns, for which he never apologised, indicated that he found the process of little worth.

At the fourth session, Steve did not appear. There was a prolonged silence at the beginning of the session; then someone queried whether anyone knew why he wasn't present. No one had any information.

After a brief pause, 'Sian', the most recent graduate of the group, abruptly stated that she hoped he would not return to the meetings. She went on to describe him as something of a 'bully' and a highly unlikeable character who rarely shared anything personal, or significant, about his life or concerns.

This sentiment was echoed by almost all those present: Steve 'wasn't empathetic', 'he was only interested in complaining', and he was not a 'team player' on shared projects, including this one.

I suspected I knew what was coming: I didn't have to wait long for confirmation. After a few minutes of these reports, Sian revealed that they had all hoped I would assist in getting Steve to leave the group; in fact, they wanted him out of their professional association as well.

I had harboured some notions about Steve's situation in the group: he didn't seem to give much, and it was nearly impossible to tell if he got anything out of the process. I thought he might do better in individual therapy before, and if, he joined another group. But people who don't get much out of the experience usually vote with their feet: I had hoped he would drop out by now. Then again, he was very awkward, but I didn't feel he was doing any damage. The participation of the others was pretty good-willed and hearty; I felt that *they were* benefitting from the group, in spite of his aggravating behaviour.

Although I felt that it was my responsibility to preserve the group, I wasn't sure that removing Steve would result in a more therapeutic effect. Was it best to eliminate the 'problem' and reflect on this without interference from that source, or should I take the risk of offering a challenge to the group that might effectively stifle productive work? Would those present consider me a coward, or irresponsible, for not excluding the disruptive member, which would give credence to their own avoidance of the situation? Or would they appreciate that other options might provide a satisfactory outcome, perhaps in ways not yet obvious?

In the first instance, I responded that the professional association was not my concern: this seemed to be agreed by all.

I then proposed that this was really a challenge for the group: what if he was excluded? How might they feel about this subsequently, even if it brought some immediate relief? Would Steve be informed as to the reason, left to his own conjectures, or was some discrete subterfuge expected on my part?

After some exchange on these queries, which gave rise to some ambivalence among the members, I proposed that they might assume some responsibility for the quality of their engagement with Steve: they were able to help each other, apparently, even with some difficult challenges. So, the not-so-easy option might be to 'get nearer', rather than distance themselves from Steve. It was, after all, *their group*; they were, and are, all constituents of this situation.

I didn't need to reveal my own reservations: they responded to the challenge willingly, if not enthusiastically. There followed a discussion about how they might broach their feelings and thoughts *about* Steve, *to* Steve. No concrete plan was put into place: just a consensus that the best course of action, for all concerned, would be to put some effort in addressing these concerns. There was a general feeling that this was the 'right' thing to do, if not the easiest.

I felt, and still do feel, that my response was a bit prescriptive: but I also thought that it was a better option for the group to at least attempt to reach out to Steve. I felt that if this endeavour was not successful, he would then take his cue and depart of his own accord. If, however, they did create a more satisfying relationship with Steve, it would be an experience that would serve them well and provide the satisfaction of meeting a challenge with 'compassion and authenticity', as they put it.

Steve never did return to the group: he sent a message that he didn't think other people were 'taking him seriously', and that it was therefore 'a waste of his time'.

I attempted to contact him by phone and left a message to invite him for a private meeting with me: there was no response. Someone else in the group claimed to have attempted to reach him via email, but there was no further report on whether he was responsive, or not.

The group used the following weeks to more deeply explore their relationships with each other, as well as those external to the group. They all regretted the missed opportunity to engage with Steve within the group context, but felt they already had a different attitude towards him and would look to explore that within the professional organisation, which was due to reconvene in a few months' time.

I felt that I had handled the ethical dilemmas reasonably well. I was able to describe some basic principles that elucidated the way I worked, and my expectations for the group, without sounding or feeling too defensive; and I also managed to provide a satisfactory rationale for not excluding someone from the group, even though it was generally acknowledged that the member did not make much of a useful contribution. I still believe the group members learned something about themselves as a result of Steve's recalcitrance: to 'do the right thing' for a fellow being was more satisfying than punitive measures, and required more courage, than simply eliminating the source of the discomfort.

The evolving situation reflected a number of the 'given' aspects of human existence, as previously described. Steve was attempting to avoid any deep or profound relationship with others, and yet, he wanted to 'belong'. This was represented in his use of the space and his physical posturing (embodiment) as a means of managing the proximity of others. He employed language to gain attention, but the words were political, rather than intentionally revealing. Paradoxically, his verbal communications disclosed quite a bit about him; his need for connection, but not for reciprocity, was evident.

Steve was choosing his behaviour, and while it was successful in managing contact with others, it came at a cost: his reticence raised resistance, and others were wary of his intentions. As with most choices, there was a gain, and a loss. By virtue of this strategy, he was partly responsible for the cynicism that was directed his way: others usually chose not to invest in anything more than a casual relationship with Steve.

Steve radically limited how he 'lived' his relationships. He cultivated a kind of inaccessibility, which made him something of a threat, as he was 'unknowable', and thus provoked uncertainty and anxiety in others. The ending of his participation with the group was one that probably suited him: a 'sudden departure', with little explanation or excuse, and a disregard of the consequences that such a withdrawal would have on others. His responsibility to others was denied by his own protective policies.

Being ethical requires an attitude: one must be willing to 'get it wrong', all or in part. It is rare in these situations that the outcome is totally satisfying: it is the careful consideration of the possible consequences, and the rationale for the choice, that generates at least some gratification.

Laws, professional codes, or ecclesiastical sources cannot provide definitive answers to ethical dilemmas: we must struggle to discover the ethical position, knowing that it, too, has its risks, consequences, and ambiguities.

## References

De Beauvoir, S. *The Ethics of Ambiguity*, 1948 (trans. B. Frachtman), Philosophical Library, New York.
Sartre, J.P. *Existentialism and Humanism*, 1973, Methuen Publishing Ltd., London.
Warnock, M. *An Intelligent Person's Guide to Ethics*, 1998, Duckworth, London.

# Chapter 33

# Conclusion and summary, Part III

This section of the book outlines some practical considerations in terms of the group therapeutic endeavour.

Most of these suggestions would be applicable to any psychotherapeutic model: here these are presented with respect to the philosophical views that have been covered in previous chapters.

Part III is titled the 'Doing and being' of the model. It has been emphasised, and it is iterated again here, that the 'doing' must be grounded in a way of 'being'; the 'being' here refers to 'being existential', certainly, and 'being-with', definitely.

The ways of dialogue chapter (Chapter 29) describes some modes of communication that foster exploration and reflection. These activities are shared among the group, and they also promote a quality of being-with essential for establishing and maintaining trusting relationships.

The effects of these pathways of dialogue are more readily apparent than the specific format of communications: these are nuanced, complementary, and even sometimes seemingly chaotic. Understanding is rarely a symmetrical or even organised process.

Resonance, presence, and the dialogical attitude are states that are ephemeral, vague, and cannot be summoned or manufactured: we can only strive to be open to such 'meetings'. What is important is the intention to be available to and for others, to allow one to respond from a deep place, and be affected.

These attitudes inform the work and extend to the reflective processes that include our dreaming state, as much as our waking one: it is suggested that these modes of being inform, reveal, and impact each other.

In the anecdotal scenarios depicted, these means of communications are sometimes apparent and at other times subtle; not every mode will be demonstrated in each vignette. Additionally, the reader may appreciate effects and communications that have not been specifically highlighted: as with all perceptions, there is a figure ground to these experiences that is relative to one's own perspective and expectations.

The last chapter proposed that the qualities of relating and the processes of reflection lend themselves as well to the notion of ethics as a 'lived' framework:

our ethical position must reflect our way of being-with-each-other and should not be subordinated to formalised standards or guidelines.

In much the same way as it is important to 'be' existential, it is similarly significant to 'be' ethical.

The 'Being and doing' referred to is in fact an inseparable paradigm: it is hoped that what has been addressed is *how* these elements are inextricably bound, much as *we* ourselves are – with each and every Other.

# Index

acceptance 133; self- 21
affinity 108
agency 56, 57, 58, 59, 109, 163
Allport, G. 43
anger 157
angst 37, 53–4, 56, 101
Anthony, E.J. 17
anxiety 53, 54–5, 56, 59, 101, 140; and
 change 84; and choice 54, 62; *see also*
 death anxiety
apartness 39
Arnold-Baker, C. 101
aspirations 84, 85, 93, 94, 132, 145, 159;
 choice and 100, 153; emotions and
 133, 139
assumptions 84, 85, 91–2, 93, 99, 132; choice
 and 100, 153; emotions and 133, 139
attitude: dialogical 97, 142, 170;
 phenomenological 35
attunement 77
authenticity 5, 23, 50–1, 58–9, 64,
 100–1, 102
autocratic leadership style 7–8, 135

Bad Faith 49, 58–9, 77
Barnes, H. 79
Barrett, W. 64, 113, 145
Becker, E. 62, 64, 71
becoming 36, 37, 46
behaviour(s): and emotion 78; *see also*
 difficult and challenging behaviours
being 40, 43, 170
'being' qualities of therapist 20–1, 23
*Being and Time* (Heidegger) 46
being-for the client 106
being-here 77
being-in-the-world 51, 72, 73, 77, 82, 86,
 90, 99, 103, 113, 114

being-towards-death 45–46, 62, 64, 67
being-with 36, 49, 50–1, 96, 97, 114, 144,
 145, 170
belonging 110, 119, 121
Bion, W. 12–15, 16, 29, 30, 31, 138;
 group mind or group culture 12; group
 as singular entity 13–14; Tavistock
 method 12
blaming 131
body: and mind 18, 72; *see also*
 embodiment
Boss, M. 47, 61, 72, 74, 102–103, 147
boundaries 120–1; time 124–6
Bracken, P. 66–7, 147
Bugental, J.F.T. 74, 79, 140

Camus, A. 71
challenging behaviour *see* difficult and
 challenging behaviours
change 27–8, 55, 56, 57, 100, 127, 128–9,
 130, 133; allowing for 63; and anxiety
 84; and choice 45; and conflict 157–8;
 group as agent of 28, 30, 130, 132;
 inevitability of 128; nature of 113; and
 responsibility 27–8; in world-view 86–8
choice 37, 44, 46–7, 55, 60, 65, 74, 100,
 113; and anxiety 54, 62; and change 45;
 freedom and 56, 57–8, 59, 63, 102, 163,
 164; 'good' 67, 164; 'responsible' 113;
 'right' 67, 100; Sartre 67, 102, 164; and
 world-view 94
closed groups 122
coercion 110, 145
cognitive dissonance 79, 86
cohesiveness, group 24, 110–11, 130, 155
Cohn, H.W. 16, 18, 30, 40, 43, 51, 59,
 63, 72, 82, 99; anxiety 54; emotions
 78; existential interpretation 144;

field theory 8–9; role of therapist 136;
  solicitude 50
collaboration 107–8
collusion 107
comfort 132–3
communication 18, 75, 113, 136, 140–6,
  170; feedback 9, 40, 51, 123, 132,
  138–9, 143–4, 155–6, 157; free 139;
  interpretation as aspect of 144–5;
  listening as mode of 142; non-verbal 75;
  possibilities for facilitation of in first
  session 140–2; reflecting back 142; self-
  disclosure 111, 118, 123–4, 144; silence
  in 145, 156; see also dialogue; language
competition 107
complicity 107
confidentiality 121, 123
conflict 85; and change 157–8; group 10,
  52, 131, 157–60
congruence 20, 22
conscious 30
consciousness 90
contracts 123
core self 23, 27
Corey, G. 13, 21
corrective recapitulation of the primary
  family group 24, 30
cosmos, values about 84, 85
counselling, and psychotherapy, distinction
  between 1
courage 132
creativity, therapist 136
cynicism 105

Dalal, F. 6, 16, 30
Dasein 39, 58, 59, 62, 67, 101
De Beauvoir, S. 163
De Maré, P. 12, 16, 17, 132
death 37, 44, 45–6, 61–5, 71, 126
death anxiety 62–5; manifestations in
  practice 64–5, 75–6
decision-making 60; ethical 164
democratic leadership style 7, 8, 135
denial 99, 100, 113
The Denial of Death (Becker) 62
dependence 12, 65
determinism 26, 30
Deurzen-Smith, E. 82
diagnostics 113
dialogical attitude 97, 142, 170
dialogue 25, 28, 96–7, 142, 170; truthful
  97, 98; see also communication

difficult and challenging behaviours
  153–162; conflict 157–60; drop-
  outs 160–1; monopolising 153–4;
  over-sharing 154–6; silence 156;
  walkouts 160
Dilthey, W. 95
disappointment 105, 128, 130, 133
disclosure see self-disclosure
disempowerment 109
dreamwork 147–52; case vignette 148–52
drop-outs 117, 160–1
DuBose, T. 37

early experiences 29
ego 15
embodiment 71–6; manifestations in
  practice 75–6; sexuality as aspect of
  74–5
emotions 77–80, 93–4, 118, 133, 139, 145;
  and behaviour 78; multiplicity of 79;
  and values 78, 93, 94, 139, 145; and
  world-view 93, 145
empathy 20–1, 22, 106
encounter groups 21–2
ending sessions 47, 142
endings 127, 133
engagement 99, 100, 105
enmity 108
essence 36, 37, 58, 67, 101
ethical stance 163–4, 170–1; case vignette
  165–9
evasion 99, 100, 113
exclusions 146, 161–2
existence 36–7, 40, 46; as both ontic and
  ontological 43, 46, 84, 99; preceding
  essence 37, 58, 67
existential factors 24, 25
existential givens 43–4, 84, 99
'exit' interviews 161
expectations 85, 91–2, 94, 99, 100, 151,
  153, 159; and emotions 133, 145
Experiences in Groups and Other Papers
  (Bion) 12
experiential learning 9–10, 26, 30,
  40, 139

facilitators see therapist(s)
facticity 46, 82
fear 56
feedback 9, 40, 51, 123, 132, 138–9,
  143–4, 155–6, 157
Feifel, H. 61

For Product Safety Concerns and Information please contact our EU
representative GPSR@taylorandfrancis.com
Taylor & Francis Verlag GmbH, Kaufingerstraße 24, 80331 München, Germany